Collins easy learning

French
Vocabulary

une autoroute

les échecs

HarperCollins Publishers
Westerhill Road
Bishopbriggs
Glasgow
G64 2QT
Great Britain

Second Edition 2012

© HarperCollins Publishers 2006, 2012

ISBN 978-0-00-748391-4

www.collins.co.uk

A catalogue record for this book is available from the British Library

Acknowledgements
We would like to thank those authors and publishers who kindly gave permission for copyright material to be used in the Collins Word Web. We would also like to thank Times Newspapers Ltd for providing valuable data.

EDITOR
Persephone Lock

CONTRIBUTORS
Gaëlle Amiot-Cadey
Laurent Jouet

BASED ON THE COLLINS GEM FRENCH
VITAL VOCAB BY
Barbara I. Christie
Màiri MacGinn
Sabine Citron
Caitlin McMahon

FOR THE PUBLISHER
Lucy Cooper
Elaine Higgleton
Susanne Reichert
Lisa Sutherland

contents

6 contents

how to use this book

The *Easy Learning French Vocabulary* is designed for both young and adult learners. Whether you are starting to learn French for the very first time, revising for school exams or simply want to brush up on your French, the *Easy Learning French Vocabulary* offers you the information you require in a clear and accessible format.

This book is divided into 50 topics, arranged in alphabetical order. This thematic approach enables you to learn related words and phrases together, so that you can become confident in using particular vocabulary in context.

Vocabulary within each topic is divided into nouns and useful phrases which are aimed at helping you to express yourself in idiomatic French. Vocabulary within each topic is graded to help you prioritize your learning. Essential words include the basic words you will need to be able to communicate effectively, important words help expand your knowledge, and useful words provide additional vocabulary which will enable you to express yourself more fully.

Nouns are grouped by gender: masculine ("le") nouns are given on the left-hand page, and feminine ("la") nouns on the right-hand page, enabling you to memorize words according to their gender. In addition, all feminine forms of adjectives are shown, as are irregular plurals and plurals of compound nouns.

At the end of the book you will find a list of supplementary vocabulary, grouped according to part of speech – adjective, verb, noun and so on. This is vocabulary which you will come across in many everyday situations.

Finally, there is an English index which lists all the essential and important nouns given under the topic headings for quick reference.

The *Easy Learning French Vocabulary* helps you to consolidate your language learning. Together with the other titles in the *Easy Learning* range you can be sure that you have all the help you need when learning French at your fingertips.

8 abbreviations

ABBREVIATIONS

adj	adjective
adv	adverb
conj	conjunction
f	feminine
inv	invariable
m	masculine
m+f	masculine and feminine form
n	noun
pl	plural
prep	preposition
qch	quelque chose
qn	quelqu'un
sb	somebody
sth	something
subj	subjunctive

The swung dash ~ is used to indicate the basic elements of the compound and appropriate endings are then added.

PHONETICS

i	as in	vie, lit
e	as in	blé, jouer
ɛ	as in	merci, très
a	as in	patte, plat
ɑ	as in	bas, gras
ɔ	as in	mort, donner
o	as in	mot, gauche
u	as in	genou, roue
y	as in	rue, tu
ø	as in	peu, deux
œ	as in	peur, meuble
ə	as in	le, premier
ɛ̃	as in	matin, plein
ɑ̃	as in	sans, vent
ɔ̃	as in	bon, ombre
œ̃	as in	brun, lundi
j	as in	yeux, pied
ɥ	as in	lui, huile
ɲ	as in	agneau, vigne
ŋ	as in	English -ing
ʃ	as in	chat, tache
ʒ	as in	je, gens
ʀ	as in	rue, venir

A colon : precedes words beginning with an aspirate **h** (**le :hibou** as opposed to **l'hippopotame**).

ESSENTIAL WORDS (*masculine*)

un	**aéroport**	airport
un	**aller-retour**	return ticket
un	**aller simple**	single ticket
un	**avion**	plane
les	**bagages**	luggage
les	**bagages à main**	hand luggage
le	**billet (d'avion)**	(plane) ticket
le	**départ**	departure
le	**douanier**	customs officer
le	**duty-free**	duty-free (shop)
	l'**horaire**	timetable
le	**numéro**	number
le	**passager**	passenger
le	**passeport**	passport
le	**prix du billet**	fare
les	**renseignements**	information
le	**retard**	delay
le	**sac**	bag
le	**taxi**	taxi
le	**touriste**	tourist
le	**vol**	flight
le	**voyage**	trip
le	**voyageur**	traveller

USEFUL PHRASES

voyager par avion to travel by plane
retenir une place d'avion to book a plane ticket
enregistrer ses bagages to check in one's luggage
l'enregistrement en ligne online check-in
j'ai manqué la correspondance I missed my connection
l'avion a décollé/a atterri the plane has taken off/has landed
le tableau des arrivées/des départs the arrivals/departures board
le vol numéro 776 en provenance de Nice/à destination de Nice flight
   number 776 from Nice/to Nice

ESSENTIAL WORDS (*feminine*)

une	**agence de voyages**	travel agent's
une	**annulation**	cancellation
une	**arrivée**	arrival
la	**carte d'identité**	ID card
la	**carte d'embarquement**	boarding card
la	**correspondance**	connection
la	**douane**	customs
une	**entrée**	entrance
une	**hôtesse de l'air**	flight attendant
la	**location de voitures**	car hire
la	**passagère**	passenger
la	**porte d'embarquement**	departure gate
la	**réduction**	reduction
la	**réservation**	reservation
la	**sortie**	exit
la	**sortie de secours**	emergency exit
les	**toilettes**	toilets
la	**touriste**	tourist
la	**valise**	suitcase

USEFUL PHRASES

récupérer ses bagages to collect one's luggage
"livraison des bagages" "baggage reclaim"
passer la douane to go through customs
j'ai quelque chose à déclarer I have something to declare
je n'ai rien à déclarer I have nothing to declare
fouiller les bagages to search the luggage
voyager en classe affaires/économique to travel business/
  economy class

IMPORTANT WORDS *(masculine)*

un **accident d'avion**	plane crash
le **billet électronique**	e-ticket
le **chariot**	trolley
un **escalier roulant**	escalator
un **hélicoptère**	helicopter
le **mal de l'air**	airsickness
le **pilote**	pilot
le **plan**	map

USEFUL WORDS *(masculine)*

un **aiguilleur du ciel**	air-traffic controller
un **atterrissage**	landing
un **avion à réaction**	jet plane
un **avion gros porteur**	jumbo jet
le **contrôle de sécurité**	security check
le **décollage**	take-off
les **droits de douane**	customs duty
l'**embarquement**	boarding
un **équipage**	crew
un **espace bébés**	mother and baby room
le **:hublot**	window
le **mur du son**	sound barrier
le **parachute**	parachute
le **portique de détection**	metal detector
le **réacteur**	jet engine
le **siège**	seat
le **steward**	flight attendant
le **tapis roulant**	moving walkway; luggage carousel
le **trou d'air**	air pocket

USEFUL PHRASES

à bord on board
horaire prévu d'arrivée/de départ estimated time of arrival/departure
"attachez vos ceintures" "fasten your seat belts"
nous survolons Londres we are flying over London
j'ai le mal de l'air I am feeling airsick
détourner un avion to hijack a plane

IMPORTANT WORDS (feminine)

la	**ceinture de sécurité**	seat belt
la	**destination**	destination
la	**durée**	length, duration
une	**horloge**	clock
la	**salle d'embarquement**	departure lounge
la	**vitesse**	speed

USEFUL WORDS (feminine)

une	**aérogare**	terminal
une	**aile**	wing
	l'**altitude**	altitude
la	**boîte noire**	black box
la	**boutique hors taxes**	duty-free shop
les	**commandes**	controls
une	**escale**	stop-over
une	**étiquette**	label
la	**:hauteur**	height
une	**hélice**	propeller
la	**compagnie aérienne**	airline
la	**piste**	runway
la	**soute**	baggage hold
la	**tour de contrôle**	control tower
la	**turbulence**	turbulence

USEFUL PHRASES

"vol AB251 pour Paris : embarquement immédiat, porte 51"
  "flight AB251 to Paris now boarding at gate 51"
nous avons fait escale à New York we stopped over in New York
un atterrissage forcé an emergency landing
un atterrissage en catastrophe a crash landing
des cigarettes hors taxes duty-free cigarettes

animals

ESSENTIAL WORDS (*masculine*)

un	**agneau**	lamb
un	**animal** (*pl* animaux)	animal
le	**bœuf** [bœf] (*pl* ~s [bø])	ox
le	**chat**	cat
le	**chaton**	kitten
le	**cheval** (*pl* chevaux)	horse
le	**chien**	dog
le	**chiot**	puppy
le	**cochon**	pig
un	**éléphant**	elephant
le	**:hamster**	hamster
le	**jardin zoologique**	zoo
le	**lapin**	rabbit
le	**lion**	lion
le	**mouton**	sheep
un	**oiseau** (*pl* -x)	bird
le	**poisson**	fish
le	**poulain**	foal
le	**tigre**	tiger
le	**veau**	calf
le	**zoo**	zoo

USEFUL PHRASES

j'aime les chats, je déteste les serpents, je préfère les souris
    I like cats, I hate snakes, I prefer mice
nous avons 12 animaux chez nous we have 12 pets (in our house)
nous n'avons pas d'animaux chez nous we have no pets (in our house)
les animaux sauvages wild animals
les animaux domestiques pets; livestock
mettre un animal en cage to put an animal in a cage
libérer un animal to set an animal free

ESSENTIAL WORDS (feminine)

la	**chatte**	cat (female)
la	**chienne**	dog (female)
la	**souris**	mouse
la	**tortue**	tortoise
la	**vache**	cow

IMPORTANT WORDS (feminine)

la	**cage**	cage
la	**queue** [kø]	tail

USEFUL PHRASES

le chien aboie the dog barks; **il grogne** it growls
le chat miaule the cat miaows; **il ronronne** it purrs
j'aime faire du cheval or **monter à cheval** I like horse-riding
à cheval on horseback
"attention, chien méchant" "beware of the dog"
"chiens interdits" "no dogs allowed"
"couché!" (to dog) "down!"
les droits des animaux animal rights

USEFUL WORDS (*masculine*)

un	**âne**	donkey
le	**bouc**	billy goat
le	**cerf** [sɛʀ]	stag
le	**chameau** (*pl* -x)	camel
le	**cochon d'Inde**	guinea-pig
le	**crapaud**	toad
le	**crocodile**	crocodile
un	**écureuil**	squirrel
le	**:hérisson**	hedgehog
un	**hippopotame**	hippopotamus
le	**kangourou**	kangaroo
le	**lièvre**	hare
le	**loup**	wolf
le	**mulet**	mule
le	**museau** (*pl* -x)	snout
un	**ours** [uʀs]	bear
un	**ours blanc**	polar bear
le	**phoque**	seal
le	**piège**	trap
le	**poil**	coat, hair
le	**poney**	pony
le	**porc** [pɔʀ]	pig
le	**renard**	fox
le	**requin**	shark
le	**rhinocéros**	rhinoceros
le	**sabot**	hoof
le	**serpent**	snake
le	**singe**	monkey
le	**taureau** (*pl* -x)	bull
le	**zèbre**	zebra

USEFUL WORDS (*feminine*)

une	**animalerie**	pet shop
la	**baleine**	whale
la	**bosse**	hump (*of camel*)
la	**carapace**	shell (*of tortoise*)
la	**chauve-souris** (*pl ~s~*)	bat
la	**chèvre**	goat
la	**corne**	horn
la	**couleuvre**	grass snake
la	**crinière**	mane
la	**défense**	tusk
la	**dinde**	turkey
la	**fourrure**	fur
la	**girafe**	giraffe
la	**grenouille**	frog
la	**griffe**	claw
la	**gueule**	mouth (*of dog, cat, lion etc*)
la	**jument**	mare
la	**lionne**	lioness
la	**mule**	mule
la	**patte**	paw
la	**poche**	pouch (*of kangaroo*)
les	**rayures**	stripes (*of zebra*)
la	**taupe**	mole
la	**tigresse**	tigress
la	**trompe**	trunk (*of elephant*)

ESSENTIAL WORDS (*masculine*)

le	**casque**	helmet
le	**cyclisme**	cycling
le	**cycliste**	cyclist
le	**frein**	brake
le	**pneu**	tyre
le	**Tour de France**	Tour de France cycle race
le	**vélo**	bike
le	**vélo tout terrain**	mountain bike
le	**VTT**	mountain bike

USEFUL WORDS (*masculine*)

un	**antivol**	padlock
le	**catadioptre**	reflector
le	**dérailleur**	derailleur
le	**garde-boue** (*pl inv*)	mudguard
le	**guidon**	handlebars
le	**moyeu** (*pl* -x)	hub
le	**pare-boue** (*pl inv*)	mudguard
le	**phare**	front light
le	**porte-bagages** (*pl inv*)	carrier
le	**rayon**	spoke
le	**réflecteur**	reflector
le	**sommet**	top (*of hill*)

USEFUL PHRASES

aller à bicyclette, aller en vélo to go by bike
je suis venu(e) en vélo I came by bike
faire du cyclisme, faire du vélo to cycle
rouler to travel
à toute vitesse at full speed
changer de vitesse to change gears
s'arrêter to stop
freiner brusquement to brake sharply

ESSENTIAL WORDS (feminine)

la	**bicyclette**	bicycle
la	**lampe**	lamp

IMPORTANT WORDS (feminine)

la	**crevaison**	puncture
la	**roue**	wheel
la	**vitesse**	speed; gear

USEFUL WORDS (feminine)

la	**barre**	crossbar
la	**chaîne**	chain
la	**côte**	slope
la	**descente**	descent
la	**dynamo**	dynamo
la	**montée**	climb
la	**pédale**	pedal
la	**pente**	slope
la	**piste cyclable**	cycle path
la	**pompe**	pump
la	**sacoche**	saddlebag
la	**selle**	saddle
la	**sonnette**	bell
la	**trousse pour crevaisons**	puncture repair kit
la	**valve**	valve

USEFUL PHRASES

faire une promenade à or **en vélo** to go for a bike ride
avoir un pneu crevé to have a flat tyre
réparer un pneu crevé to mend a puncture
la roue avant/arrière the front/back wheel
gonfler les pneus to blow up the tyres
brillant(e), reluisant(e) shiny
rouillé(e) rusty
fluorescent(e) fluorescent

ESSENTIAL WORDS (*masculine*)

le **canard**	duck
le **ciel**	sky
le **coq**	cock
le **dindon**	turkey
un **oiseau** (*pl* -x)	bird
le **perroquet**	parrot

USEFUL WORDS (*masculine*)

un **aigle**	eagle
le **bec**	beak
le **choucas**	jackdaw
le **coq de bruyère**	grouse
le **corbeau** (*pl* -x)	raven
le **coucou**	cuckoo
le **cygne** [siɲ]	swan
un **étourneau** (*pl* -x)	starling
le **faisan**	pheasant
le **faucon**	falcon
le **:hibou** (*pl* -x)	owl
le **martin-pêcheur** (*pl* ~s~s)	kingfisher
le **merle**	blackbird
le **moineau** (*pl* -x)	sparrow
le **nid**	nest
un **œuf**	egg
le **paon** [pã]	peacock
le **pic**	woodpecker
le **pigeon**	pigeon
le **pingouin**	penguin
le **rapace**	bird of prey
le **roitelet**	wren
le **rossignol**	nightingale
le **rouge-gorge** (*pl* ~s~s)	robin
le **serin**	canary
le **vautour**	vulture

ESSENTIAL WORDS (feminine)

une	**oie**	goose
la	**perruche**	budgie
la	**poule**	hen

USEFUL WORDS (feminine)

une	**aile**	wing
une	**alouette**	lark
une	**autruche**	ostrich
la	**cage**	cage
la	**caille**	quail
la	**cigogne**	stork
la	**colombe**	dove
la	**corneille**	crow
la	**grive**	thrush
une	**hirondelle**	swallow
la	**mésange bleue**	bluetit
la	**mouette**	seagull
la	**perdrix** [pɛRdRi]	partridge
la	**pie**	magpie
la	**plume**	feather

USEFUL PHRASES

voler to fly
s'envoler to fly away
faire son nid to build a nest
siffler to whistle
chanter to sing
mettre un oiseau en cage to put a bird in a cage
pondre un œuf to lay an egg
un oiseau migrateur a migratory bird

ESSENTIAL WORDS (*masculine*)

le	**bras**	arm
les	**cheveux**	hair
le	**cœur**	heart
le	**corps** [kɔʀ]	body
le	**doigt**	finger
le	**dos**	back
	l'**estomac** [ɛstɔma]	stomach
le	**genou** (*pl* -x)	knee
le	**nez**	nose
un	**œil** (*pl* yeux)	eye
le	**pied**	foot
le	**ventre**	stomach
le	**visage**	face
les	**yeux**	eyes

IMPORTANT WORDS (*masculine*)

le	**cou**	neck
le	**front**	forehead
le	**menton**	chin
le	**pouce**	thumb
le	**sang**	blood
le	**sourcil** [suʀsi]	eyebrow

USEFUL PHRASES

debout standing
assis(e) sitting
couché(e) lying
je vais me faire couper les cheveux I am going to have my hair cut

ESSENTIAL WORDS (feminine)

la	**bouche**	mouth
la	**dent**	tooth
la	**gorge**	throat
la	**jambe**	leg
la	**main**	hand
une	**oreille**	ear
la	**tête**	head

IMPORTANT WORDS (feminine)

la	**cheville**	ankle
une	**épaule**	shoulder
la	**figure**	face
la	**joue**	cheek
la	**langue**	tongue
la	**peau**	skin
la	**poitrine**	chest, bust
la	**voix**	voice

USEFUL PHRASES

grand(e) tall, big
petit(e) small, short
gros(se) fat
maigre skinny
mince slim
joli(e) pretty
laid(e) ugly
mignon(ne) cute

USEFUL WORDS *(masculine)*

le **cerveau**	brain
le **cil** [sil]	eyelash
le **coude**	elbow
le **derrière**	bottom
les **doigts de pied**	toes
le **foie**	liver
le **geste**	gesture
le **gros orteil**	the big toe
un **index**	forefinger
le **mollet**	calf (*of leg*)
le **muscle**	muscle
un **ongle**	nail
un **orteil**	toe
un **os** [ɔs] (*pl* ~ [o])	bone
le **poignet**	wrist
le **poing**	fist
le **poumon**	lung
le **rein**	kidney
le **sein**	breast
le **squelette**	skeleton
le **talon**	heel
le **teint**	complexion
les **traits**	features

USEFUL PHRASES

se moucher to blow one's nose
se couper les ongles to cut one's nails
se faire couper les cheveux to have one's hair cut
hausser les épaules to shrug one's shoulders
faire oui/non de la tête to nod/shake one's head
voir to see; **entendre** to hear; **se sentir** to feel;
sentir to smell; **toucher** to touch; **goûter** to taste;
serrer la main à qn to shake hands with sb
faire bonjour/au revoir de la main à qn to wave hello/goodbye to sb
montrer qch du doigt to point at sth

USEFUL WORDS *(feminine)*

une	**artère**	artery
la	**chair**	flesh
la	**colonne vertébrale**	spine
la	**côte**	rib
la	**cuisse**	thigh
la	**:hanche**	hip
la	**lèvre**	lip
la	**mâchoire**	jaw
la	**nuque**	nape of the neck
la	**paupière**	eyelid
la	**plante du pied**	sole of the foot
la	**prunelle**	pupil (*of the eye*)
la	**taille**	waist; size
la	**tempe**	temple
la	**veine**	vein

USEFUL PHRASES

tour de hanches hip measurement
tour de taille waist measurement
tour de poitrine chest measurement
sourd(e) deaf
aveugle blind
muet(te) dumb
handicapé(e) with a disability
il est plus grand que toi he is taller than you
elle a beaucoup grandi she has grown a lot
je me trouve trop gros I think I am overweight
elle a grossi/maigri she has put on/lost weight
elle fait 1,47 mètres she is 1.47 metres tall
il pèse 40 kilos he weighs 40 kilos

SEASONS

le	**printemps**	spring
	l'**été** (m)	summer
	l'**automne** (m)	autumn
	l'**hiver** (m)	winter

MONTHS

janvier	January	**juillet**	July
février	February	**août**	August
mars	March	**septembre**	September
avril	April	**octobre**	October
mai	May	**novembre**	November
juin	June	**décembre**	December

DAYS OF THE WEEK

lundi	Monday
mardi	Tuesday
mercredi	Wednesday
jeudi	Thursday
vendredi	Friday
samedi	Saturday
dimanche	Sunday

USEFUL PHRASES
au printemps in spring
en été/automne/hiver in summer/autumn/winter
en mai in May
le 10 juillet 2015 on 10 July 2015
nous sommes le 3 décembre it's 3 December
le samedi, je vais à la piscine on Saturdays I go to the swimming pool
samedi je suis allé à la piscine on Saturday I went to the swimming pool
samedi prochain/dernier next/last Saturday
le samedi précédent/suivant the previous/following Saturday

CALENDAR

le **calendrier**	calendar
le **jour**	day
la **saison**	season
la **semaine**	week
le **mois**	month
les **jours de la semaine**	days of the week
le **jour férié**	public holiday
le **weekend**	weekend

USEFUL PHRASES

le premier avril April Fools' Day
le premier mai May Day
le quatorze juillet Bastille Day (French national holiday)
le dimanche de Pâques Easter Sunday
le lundi de Pâques Easter Monday
mercredi des Cendres Ash Wednesday
vendredi saint Good Friday
le jour de l'An New Year's Day
le réveillon du jour de l'An New Year's Eve dinner *or* party
l'Avent (*m*) Advent
le Carême Lent
la Marseillaise the Marseillaise (French national anthem)
Noël (*m*) Christmas
à Noël at Christmas
le jour de Noël Christmas Day
la veille de Noël, la nuit de Noël Christmas Eve
Pâques (*fpl*) Easter
le jour de Pâques Easter Day
la Pâque juive Passover
le poisson d'avril April fool's trick
le Ramadan Ramadan
la Saint-Sylvestre New Year's Eve
la Saint-Valentin St Valentine's Day
la Toussaint All Saints' Day

ESSENTIAL WORDS (*masculine*)

un	**anniversaire**	birthday
un	**anniversaire de mariage**	wedding anniversary
le	**cadeau** (*pl* -x)	present
le	**mariage**	wedding
le	**rendez-vous** (*pl inv*)	appointment, date

IMPORTANT WORDS (*masculine*)

le	**festival**	festival
le	**feu d'artifice**	firework; firework display
le	**feu de joie**	bonfire

USEFUL WORDS (*masculine*)

le	**baptême**	christening
le	**cimetière**	cemetery
le	**décès**	death
le	**défilé**	procession; march
un	**enterrement**	funeral
le	**faire-part (de mariage)** (*pl inv*)	wedding invitation
le	**témoin**	witness

USEFUL PHRASES

fêter son anniversaire to celebrate one's birthday
ma sœur est née en 1995 my sister was born in 1995
elle vient d'avoir 17 ans she's just turned 17
il m'a offert ce cadeau he gave me this present
je te l'offre! I'm giving it to you!
je vous remercie thank you
divorcer to get divorced
se marier to get married
se fiancer (avec qn) to get engaged (to sb)
mon père est mort il y a deux ans my father died two years ago
enterrer, ensevelir to bury

ESSENTIAL WORDS *(feminine)*

la **date**	date
la **fête**	saint's day; festival; fair; party

IMPORTANT WORDS *(feminine)*

les **festivités**	festivities
la **fête foraine**	fun fair
les **fiançailles**	engagement
la **foire**	fair
la **mort**	death
la **naissance**	birth

USEFUL WORDS *(feminine)*

la **carte de vœux**	greetings card
la **cérémonie**	ceremony
la **demoiselle d'honneur**	bridesmaid
les **étrennes**	New Year's gift
la **fête folklorique**	folk festival
la **lune de miel**	honeymoon
les **noces**	wedding
la **retraite**	retirement

USEFUL PHRASES

les noces d'argent/d'or/de diamant silver/golden/diamond wedding anniversary

souhaiter la bonne année à qn to wish sb a happy New Year

faire une fête to have a party

inviter ses amis to invite one's friends

choisir un cadeau to choose a gift

joyeux Noël! Happy Christmas!

bon anniversaire! happy birthday!

tous mes vœux best wishes

ESSENTIAL WORDS (*masculine*)

le **bloc sanitaire**	washrooms
le **campeur**	camper
le **camping**	camping; campsite
le **canif**	penknife
le **couteau** (*pl* -x)	knife
le **dépôt de butane**	butane store
un **emplacement**	pitch, site
le **feu de camp**	campfire
le **gardien**	warden
le **gaz**	gas
le **lavabo**	washbasin
le **lit de camp**	camp bed
le **mobile home**	motorhome
le **supplément**	extra charge
le **terrain de camping**	campsite
le **véhicule**	vehicle
les **WC**	toilets

IMPORTANT WORDS (*masculine*)

le **barbecue**	barbecue
le **matelas pneumatique**	airbed
un **ouvre-boîtes**	tin-opener
le **réchaud**	stove
le **règlement**	rules
le **sac à dos**	rucksack
le **sac de couchage**	sleeping bag
le **tire-bouchon** (*pl* ~s)	corkscrew

USEFUL PHRASES

faire du camping to go camping
camper to camp
bien aménagé(e) well equipped
faire un feu to make a fire

ESSENTIAL WORDS (feminine)

une	allumette	match
une	assiette	plate
la	boîte	tin, can; box
les	boîtes de conserve	tinned food
la	campeuse	camper
la	caravane	caravan
la	chaise longue	deckchair
la	cuiller, la cuillère	spoon
la	douche	shower
	l'eau non potable	non-drinking water
	l'eau potable	drinking water
la	fourchette	fork
la	glace	mirror
la	lampe électrique	torch
la	lampe de poche	torch
la	machine à laver	washing machine
la	nuit	night
la	piscine	swimming pool
la	poubelle	dustbin
la	salle	room; hall
la	table	table
la	tente	tent
les	toilettes	toilets

IMPORTANT WORDS (feminine)

les	installations sanitaires	washing facilities
la	laverie	launderette
la	lessive	washing powder; washing
	l'ombre	shade; shadow
la	prise de courant	socket
la	salle de jeux	games room

USEFUL PHRASES

dresser or **monter une tente** to pitch a tent
griller des saucisses to grill some sausages

ESSENTIAL WORDS (*masculine*)

un	**agent (de police)**	policeman
un	**agriculteur**	farmer
un	**artisan**	self-employed craftsman
le	**boulot**	job
le	**bureau** (*pl* -x)	office
le	**caissier**	check-out assistant
le	**chauffeur de taxi**	taxi driver
le	**conseiller d'orientation**	careers adviser
le	**designer web**	web designer
le	**développeur**	developer
un	**électricien**	electrician
un	**employé**	employee
un	**employeur**	employer
un	**enseignant**	teacher
le	**facteur**	postman
le	**garagiste**	mechanic; garage owner
un	**infirmier**	(male) nurse
un	**informaticien**	computer scientist
le	**mécanicien**	mechanic; engineer; train driver
le	**médecin** (*m+f*)	doctor
le	**métier**	trade
le	**patron**	boss
le	**pharmacien**	chemist
le	**pompier**	firefighter
le	**professeur**	teacher
le	**programmeur**	programmer
le	**salaire**	wages
le	**soldat**	soldier
le	**steward**	flight attendant
le	**travail**	work
le	**vendeur**	salesman, shop assistant

USEFUL PHRASES

intéressant(e)/peu intéressant(e) interesting/not very interesting
il est facteur he is a postman
il/elle est médecin he/she is a doctor
travailler to work
devenir to become

ESSENTIAL WORDS *(feminine)*

une	**agricultrice**	farmer
une	**ambition**	ambition
une	**artisane**	self-employed craftswoman
la	**banque**	bank
la	**caissière**	check-out assistant
la	**conseillère d'orientation**	careers adviser
la	**dactylo**	typist
la	**développeuse**	developer
une	**employée**	employee
une	**enseignante**	teacher
la	**factrice**	postwoman
une	**hôtesse de l'air**	flight attendant
une	**industrie**	industry
une	**infirmière**	nurse
une	**informaticienne**	computer scientist
la	**patronne**	boss
la	**professeur**	teacher
la	**profession**	profession
la	**programmeuse**	programmer
la	**réceptionniste**	receptionist
la	**retraite**	retirement
la	**secrétaire**	secretary
une	**usine**	factory
la	**vedette** *(m+f)*	star
la	**vendeuse**	shop assistant
la	**vie active**	working life

USEFUL PHRASES

travailler pour gagner sa vie to work for one's living
mon ambition est d'être juge it is my ambition to be a judge
que faites-vous dans la vie? what is your job?
postuler à un emploi to apply for a job

IMPORTANT WORDS (*masculine*)

un **apprentissage**	apprenticeship
l'**avenir**	future
le **CDD**	fixed term contract
le **CDI**	permanent contract
le **chef**	boss
le **chômage**	unemployment
le **chômeur**	unemployed person
le **coiffeur**	hairdresser
le **collègue**	colleague
le **commerçant**	shopkeeper
le **commerce**	business
le **concierge**	caretaker
le **contrat**	contract
le **décorateur**	decorator
un **emploi**	job
un **entretien (d'embauche)**	(job) interview
le **gérant**	manager
un **homme d'affaires**	businessman
un **intérimaire**	temp
le **marché du travail**	job market
un **opticien**	optician
un **ouvrier**	worker
le **peintre**	painter
le **pilote**	pilot
le **plombier**	plumber
le **président**	president; chairman
le **salarié**	wage-earner
le **sapeur-pompier** (*pl* ~s~s)	firefighter
le **syndicat**	trade union

USEFUL PHRASES

être au chômage to be unemployed
licencier qn to make sb redundant
l'**emploi saisonnier** seasonal work
"**offres d'emplois**" "situations vacant"
être syndiqué to be in a union
gagner 150 livres par semaine to earn £150 a week

IMPORTANT WORDS *(feminine)*

les	**affaires**	business
une	**agence d'intérim**	temping agency
	l'**ANPE**	job centre
une	**augmentation**	rise
la	**candidature**	application
la	**carrière**	career
la	**coiffeuse**	hairdresser
la	**collègue**	colleague
la	**concierge**	caretaker
la	**cuisinière**	cook
une	**entrevue**	interview
la	**femme d'affaires**	businesswoman
la	**femme de ménage**	cleaner
la	**gérante**	manageress
la	**grève**	strike
une	**intérimaire**	temp
la	**lettre de motivation**	covering letter
une	**ouvrière**	worker
la	**peintre**	painter
la	**politique**	politics
la	**présidente**	president; chairwoman
la	**salariée**	wage-earner
la	**situation**	job; situation

USEFUL PHRASES

une augmentation de salaire a pay rise
se mettre en grève to go on strike
faire la grève to be on strike
travailler à plein temps/à mi-temps to work full-time/part-time
faire des heures supplémentaires to work overtime
la réduction du temps de travail reduction in working hours

USEFUL WORDS *(masculine)*

un	**animateur**	activity leader
un	**architecte**	architect
un	**artiste**	artist
un	**avocat**	lawyer
le	**cadre**	executive
le	**chercheur**	researcher
le	**chirurgien**	surgeon
le	**comptable**	accountant
le	**couturier**	fashion designer
le	**député**	MP
un	**écrivain**	writer
le	**fonctionnaire**	civil servant
un	**homme politique**	politician
un	**horaire**	schedule
un	**ingénieur**	engineer
un	**interprète**	interpreter
le	**journaliste**	journalist
le	**juge**	judge
le	**maçon**	mason
le	**mannequin** *(m+f)*	model *(person)*
le	**marin**	sailor; seaman
le	**menuisier**	joiner
le	**notaire**	lawyer, solicitor
le	**personnel**	staff
le	**photographe**	photographer
le	**présentateur télé**	TV presenter
le	**président-directeur général, le PDG**	chairman and managing director
le	**prêtre**	priest
le	**rédacteur**	editor
le	**représentant**	rep
le	**stage en entreprise**	work placement
le	**stage de formation**	training course
le	**traducteur**	translator
le	**vétérinaire** *(m+f)*	vet
le	**vigneron**	wine grower
le	**VRP**	sales rep

USEFUL WORDS *(feminine)*

une	**animatrice**	activity leader
une	**artiste**	artist
une	**avocate**	lawyer
la	**comptable**	accountant
la	**couturière**	dressmaker
une	**entreprise**	business
la	**femme-agent**	policewoman
la	**femme au foyer**	housewife
la	**fonctionnaire**	civil servant
la	**formation**	training
la	**formation continue**	in-house training
la	**grève du zèle**	work-to-rule
la	**grève perlée**	go-slow
une	**indemnité de chômage**	unemployment benefit
une	**indemnité de licenciement**	redundancy payment
une	**interprète**	interpreter
la	**journaliste**	journalist
	l'**orientation professionnelle**	careers guidance
la	**présentatrice télé**	TV presenter
la	**rédactrice**	editor
la	**religieuse**	nun
la	**représentante**	rep
la	**société**	company
la	**traductrice**	translator

USEFUL PHRASES

un emploi temporaire/permanent a temporary/permanent job
être engagé(e) to be taken on
être renvoyé(e) to be dismissed
mettre qn à la porte to give sb the sack
un emploi à mi-temps a part-time job
chercher du travail to look for work
faire un stage de formation to go on a training course
pointer to clock in *or* out
avoir un horaire flexible to work flexitime
travailler à son compte to be self-employed
travailler dans l'informatique/le tourisme to work in computing/tourism

ESSENTIAL WORDS *(masculine)*

un **agent (de police)**	policeman
l'**auto-stop**, le **stop**	hitch-hiking
un **auto-stoppeur** *(pl ~s)*	hitch-hiker
le **bouchon**	traffic jam
le **camion**	lorry, truck
le **carrefour**	crossroads
le **chauffeur** *(m+f)*	driver; chauffeur
le **conducteur**	driver
le **cycliste**	cyclist
le **diesel**	diesel
le **feu rouge**	traffic lights, red light
les **feux**	traffic lights
le **frein**	brake
le **garage**	garage
le **garagiste**	mechanic; garage owner
le **gas-oil**	diesel (oil)
le **kilomètre**	kilometre
le **litre**	litre
le **mécanicien**	mechanic
le **numéro**	number
le **parking**	car park
le **péage**	toll
le **permis de conduire**	driving licence
le **piéton**	pedestrian
le **plan (de la ville)**	street map
le **pneu**	tyre
le **radar**	speed camera
le **voyage**	journey

USEFUL PHRASES

faire du stop, faire de l'auto-stop to hitch-hike
s'arrêter au feu rouge to stop at the red light
freiner brusquement to brake sharply
100 kilomètres à l'heure, 100 kilomètres-heure 100 kilometres an hour
crever, avoir un pneu crevé to have a puncture
as-tu ton permis? do you have a driving licence?

ESSENTIAL WORDS (feminine)

une	**auto**	car
une	**automobile**	car
une	**autoroute**	motorway
une	**autoroute à péage**	toll motorway
une	**auto-stoppeuse** (pl ~s)	hitch-hiker
la	**caravane**	caravan
la	**carte grise**	(car) registration document
la	**carte routière**	road map
la	**carte verte**	insurance certificate
la	**conductrice**	driver
la	**déviation**	diversion
la	**direction**	direction
la	**direction assistée**	power steering
la	**distance**	distance
l'	**eau**	water
l'	**essence**	petrol
l'	**essence sans plomb**	unleaded petrol
l'	**huile**	oil
la	**police**	police
la	**route**	road
la	**route nationale**	main road
la	**station-service** (pl ~s)	petrol station
la	**voiture**	car

USEFUL PHRASES

on va faire une promenade en voiture we're going for a drive (in the car)
le plein, s'il vous plaît fill her up please!
prenez la route de Lyon take the road to Lyons
c'est un voyage de 3 heures it's a 3-hour journey
bonne route! have a good journey!
allez, en route! let's go!
en route nous avons vu ... on the way we saw ...
doubler or **dépasser une voiture** to overtake a car
se garer to park (the car)
réparer to fix

IMPORTANT WORDS (*masculine*)

un	**accident (de la route)**	(road) accident
un	**alcootest**	Breathalyzer® test
un	**automobiliste**	motorist
le	**camionneur**	lorry driver
le	**carburant**	petrol
le	**code de la route**	highway code
le	**coffre**	boot
le	**contrôle technique**	MOT test
un	**embouteillage**	traffic jam
l'	**embrayage**	clutch
un	**éthylotest**	Breathalyzer® kit
le	**gilet de sécurité**	high-vis vest
le	**klaxon**	horn
le	**lavage**	(car) wash
le	**moteur**	engine
les	**papiers**	official papers
le	**phare**	headlight
le	**pompiste**	petrol pump attendant
le	**rond-point** (*pl* ~s~s)	roundabout
le	**sens unique**	one-way street
le	**stationnement**	parking
le	**télépéage**	toll prepayment system
le	**triangle de pré-signalisation**	warning triangle

USEFUL PHRASES

d'abord on met le moteur en marche first you switch on the engine
le moteur démarre the engine starts up
la voiture démarre the car moves off
on roule we're driving along
accélérer to accelerate
continuer to continue
ralentir to slow down
s'arrêter to stop
stationner to park; to be parked
couper le moteur to switch off the engine
il y a eu un accident there's been an accident
vos papiers, s'il vous plaît may I see your papers please?

IMPORTANT WORDS *(feminine)*

une	**amende**	fine
une	**assurance**	insurance
une	**auto-école** *(pl ~s)*	driving school
une	**automobiliste**	motorist
la	**batterie**	battery
la	**carrosserie**	bodywork
la	**ceinture de sécurité**	seat belt
la	**circulation**	traffic
la	**collision**	collision
la	**crevaison**	puncture
la	**frontière**	border
la	**marque**	make (*of car*)
la	**panne**	breakdown
la	**pièce de rechange**	spare part
la	**police d'assurance**	insurance policy
la	**pompe à essence**	petrol pump
la	**portière**	(car) door
la	**priorité**	right of way
la	**roue**	wheel
la	**roue de secours**	spare wheel
la	**vitesse**	speed; gear
la	**voiture de dépannage**	breakdown van
la	**voiture éléctrique/hybride**	electric/hybrid car
la	**zone bleue**	restricted parking zone

USEFUL PHRASES

être en panne d'essence to run out of petrol
aux heures d'affluence at rush hour
il a eu 150 euros d'amende he got a 150-euro fine
êtes-vous assuré(e)? are you insured?
n'oubliez pas de mettre vos ceintures don't forget to put on your seat belts
à la frontière at the border
être *or* **tomber en panne** to break down
je suis tombé(e) en panne sèche I've run out of petrol
la roue avant/arrière the front/back wheel

USEFUL WORDS (*masculine*)

un	**accélérateur**	accelerator
un	**apprenti conducteur**	learner driver
un	**arrêt d'urgence**	emergency stop
le	**blessé**	casualty
le	**capot**	bonnet
le	**carburateur**	carburettor
le	**clignotant**	indicator
le	**compteur de vitesse**	speedometer
le	**contractuel**	traffic warden
le	**démarreur**	starter
le	**détour**	detour
un	**essuie-glace** (*pl inv*)	windscreen wiper
le	**lavage auto**	car-wash
le	**moniteur d'auto-école**	driving instructor
le	**motard**	motorcycle policeman; motorcyclist
le	**panneau** (*pl* -x)	road sign
le	**parcmètre**	parking meter
le	**pare-brise** (*pl inv*)	windscreen
le	**pare-chocs** (*pl inv*)	bumper
le	**périphérique**	ring road
le	**pot catalytique**	catalytic converter
le	**PV**	fine
le	**rétroviseur**	rear-view mirror
le	**routier**	long-distance lorry driver
le	**starter**	choke
le	**système de navigation GPS**	satellite navigation system; GPS
le	**virage**	bend
le	**volant**	steering wheel

USEFUL PHRASES

l'accident a fait 6 blessés/morts 6 people were injured/killed in the accident

il faut faire un détour we have to make a detour

une contravention pour excès de vitesse a fine for speeding

dresser un PV à un conducteur to book a driver

USEFUL WORDS (feminine)

une	**agglomération**	built-up area
une	**aire de services**	service area
une	**aire de stationnement**	lay-by
une	**apprentie conductrice**	learner driver
une	**auto-école**	driving school
la	**bande d'arrêt d'urgence**	hard shoulder
la	**bande médiane**	central reservation
la	**boîte de vitesses**	gearbox
la	**bretelle de raccordement**	slip road
la	**conduite accompagnée**	*driving as a learner accompanied by an experienced driver*
la	**consommation d'essence**	petrol consumption
la	**contractuelle**	traffic warden
la	**contravention**	traffic offence
la	**dépanneuse**	breakdown van
la	**file**	lane
la	**galerie**	roof rack
la	**leçon de conduite**	driving lesson
la	**limitation de vitesse**	speed limit
la	**pédale**	pedal
la	**plaque d'immatriculation** *or* **minéralogique**	number plate
la	**pression**	pressure
la	**remorque**	trailer
la	**routière**	long-distance lorry driver
la	**voie**	way, road; lane *(on road)*
la	**voie de raccordement**	slip road

USEFUL PHRASES

"priorité à droite" "give way to the right"
"serrez à droite" "keep to the right"
"accès interdit" "no entry"
"stationnement interdit" "no parking"
"travaux" "roadworks"

ESSENTIAL WORDS (*masculine*)

un	**anorak**	anorak
le	**bouton**	button
le	**caleçon**	boxer shorts
le	**chapeau** (*pl* -x)	hat
le	**col**	collar
le	**collant**	tights
le	**complet**	suit
le	**costume**	suit (*for man*); costume
un	**imper(méable)**	raincoat
le	**jean** [dʒin]	jeans
le	**maillot (de bain)**	swimming trunks *or* swimsuit
le	**manteau** (*pl* -x)	coat
le	**mouchoir**	handkerchief
le	**pantalon**	trousers
le	**parapluie**	umbrella
le	**pardessus**	overcoat
le	**pull-over, le pull** [pyl(ɔvœʀ)]	jumper
le	**pyjama**	pyjamas
le	**sac**	bag
le	**slip de bain**	swimming trunks
le	**slip**	pants
le	**soulier**	shoe
les	**sous-vêtements**	underwear
le	**T-shirt, le tee-shirt**	T-shirt
les	**vêtements**	clothes

IMPORTANT WORDS (*masculine*)

le	**blouson**	jacket
le	**chemisier**	blouse
le	**gant**	glove
le	**sac à main**	handbag
le	**short** [ʃɔʀt]	shorts
le	**tricot**	jumper
un	**uniforme**	uniform
le	**veston**	jacket (*for man*)

ESSENTIAL WORDS *(feminine)*

la	**capuche**	hood
la	**chaussette**	sock
la	**chaussure**	shoe
la	**chemise**	shirt
la	**chemise de nuit**	nightdress
la	**cravate**	tie
la	**culotte**	knickers
la	**jupe**	skirt
la	**mode**	fashion
la	**parka**	parka
la	**pointure**	(shoe) size
la	**robe**	dress
la	**sandale**	sandal
la	**taille**	size; waist
la	**veste**	jacket

IMPORTANT WORDS *(feminine)*

la	**botte**	boot
la	**ceinture**	belt
la	**pantoufle**	slipper
la	**poche**	pocket

USEFUL PHRASES

le matin je m'habille in the morning I get dressed
le soir je me déshabille in the evening I get undressed
porter to wear
mettre to put on
quand je rentre du lycée je me change when I get home from school I get changed
à la mode fashionable
démodé(e) old-fashioned
cela fait très chic that's very smart
cela vous va bien that suits you
quelle est votre taille? what size do you take?
quelle est votre pointure? what shoe size do you take?
je chausse du 38 I take size 38 in shoes

USEFUL WORDS (*masculine*)

les	accessoires	accessories
les	bas	stockings
les	baskets	trainers
le	béret	beret
le	bermuda	Bermuda shorts
le	bibi	fascinator
le	bleu de travail	overalls
le	bonnet	(woolly) hat
le	chandail	(thick) jumper
le	chapeau (*pl* -x) melon	bowler hat
le	collant	tights
le	débardeur	tank top
le	défilé	fashion show
le	foulard	scarf
le	gilet de corps	vest
le	gilet	waistcoat; cardigan
les	:hauts talons	high heels
le	jupon	underskirt
les	lacets	(shoe)laces
le	linge	washing
le	nettoyage à sec	dry-cleaning
le	nœud papillon	bow tie
le	pantacourt	three-quarter length trousers
le	polo	polo shirt
le	ruban	ribbon
le	sac à bandoulière	shoulder bag
le	soutien-gorge (*pl* ~s~)	bra
le	survêtement	tracksuit
le	sweat [swɛt]	sweatshirt
le	sweat à capuche	hooded top
le	tablier	apron
le	tailleur	woman's suit
les	talons aiguilles	stiletto heels
le	tricot de corps	vest

USEFUL WORDS *(feminine)*

la	**boutonnière**	buttonhole
les	**bretelles**	braces
la	**cabine d'essayage**	fitting room
la	**canne**	walking stick
la	**casquette**	cap
la	**combinaison**	slip
la	**doudoune**	down jacket
une	**écharpe**	scarf
une	**espadrille**	espadrille
la	**fermeture éclair**	zip
la	**:haute couture**	haute couture
la	**jupe-culotte** (*pl ~s~s*)	culottes
la	**manche**	sleeve
la	**polaire**	fleece
la	**robe de chambre**	dressing gown
la	**robe de mariée**	wedding dress
la	**robe du soir**	evening dress (*for woman*)
la	**salopette**	dungarees
la	**tong**	flip flop

USEFUL PHRASES

long(ue) long
court(e) short
une robe à manches courtes/longues a short-sleeved/long-sleeved dress
serré(e) tight
ample loose
une jupe serrée a tight skirt
rayé(e) striped
à carreaux checked
à pois spotted
les vêtements sport casual clothes
en tenue de soirée in evening dress
à la mode fashionable
branché(e) trendy
démodé(e) old-fashioned

beige	beige
blanc (blanche)	white
bleu(e)	blue
bordeaux	maroon
brun(e)	brown
doré(e)	golden
fauve	fawn
gris(e)	grey
jaune	yellow
marron	brown
mauve	mauve
noir(e)	black
orange, orangé(e)	orange
rose	pink
rouge	red
turquoise	turquoise
vert(e)	green
violet (violette)	violet, purple
bleu clair	pale blue
bleu foncé	dark blue
rouge vif	bright red
bleu ciel	sky blue
bleu marine	navy blue
bleu roi	royal blue

USEFUL PHRASES

la couleur colour
de quelle couleur sont tes yeux/tes cheveux? what colour are your eyes/ is your hair?
le bleu te va bien blue suits you; the blue one suits you
peindre qch en bleu to paint sth blue
des chaussures bleues blue shoes
des chaussures bleu clair light blue shoes
elle a les yeux verts she has green eyes
changer de couleur to change colour
la Maison Blanche the White House
blanc comme neige as white as snow
Blanche-Neige Snow White
un steak bleu a very rare steak, an underdone steak
le Petit Chaperon rouge Little Red Riding Hood
rougir to turn red
rougir de honte to blush with shame
pâle comme un linge as white as a sheet
tout(e) bronzé(e) as brown as a berry
il était couvert de bleus he was black and blue
un œil au beurre noir a black eye

ESSENTIAL WORDS *(masculine)*

un **ordinateur**	computer
un **ordinateur portable**	laptop
le **PC**	PC, personal computer
le **programme**	program

USEFUL WORDS *(masculine)*

le **blogue**	blog
le **blogueur**	blogger
le **clavier**	keyboard
le **curseur**	cursor
le **document**	document
un **écran (tactile)**	(touch) screen
le **fichier**	file
le **gaming**	gaming
le **:haut débit**	broadband
l'**Internet**	internet
le **jeu vidéo**	computer game
le **livre électronique**	e-book
le **logiciel**	software
le **mail**	email
les **médias sociaux**	social media
le **menu**	menu
le **microblogue**	microblog
le **moniteur**	monitor
le **navigateur**	browser
le **nom d'utilisateur**	username
le **nuage de tags**	cloud
le **pirate**	hacker
le **post**	post *(on forum or blog)*
le **réseau**	network
le **sans-fil**	wireless
le **serveur**	server
le **site de réseautage**	social networking site
le **site Web**	website
le **système d'exploitation**	operating system
le **virus**	virus
le **Web**	web
le **webmail**	webmail
le **wifi**	wifi

ESSENTIAL WORDS *(feminine)*

une **imprimante**	printer
l'**informatique**	computer science; computer studies
la **souris**	mouse
la **tablette**	tablet

USEFUL WORDS *(feminine)*

une **adresse électronique**	email address
une **appli**	app
une **application**	program
la **base de données**	database
la **blogueuse**	blogger
la **cartouche d'encre**	ink cartridge
la **clé électronique**	dongle
la **clé USB**	USB key
la **connexion Internet**	internet connection
la **console de jeu**	games console
la **corbeille**	recycle bin
les **données**	data
la **fenêtre**	window
la **fonction**	function
une **icône**	icon
l'**informatique en nuage**	cloud computing
une **interface**	interface
une **internaute**	internet user
la **manette**	joystick
la **mémoire**	memory
la **page d'accueil**	home page
la **sauvegarde**	back-up
la **touche**	key
la **webcam**	webcam

USEFUL PHRASES

taper, saisir to key; **copier** to copy
effacer to delete; **enregistrer** to save
imprimer to print
surfer sur Internet to surf the internet
faire les achats en ligne to shop online
télécharger un fichier to download *or* upload a file

COUNTRIES

ESSENTIAL WORDS (*masculine*)

le	**Canada**	Canada
les	**États-Unis**	United States
le	**pays**	country
les	**Pays-Bas**	Netherlands
le	**pays de Galles**	Wales
le	**Royaume-Uni**	United Kingdom
les	**USA**	USA

USEFUL WORDS (*masculine*)

le	**Danemark**	Denmark
l'	**Hexagone**	France
le	**Japon**	Japan
le	**Maroc**	Morocco
le	**Pakistan**	Pakistan
le	**tiers-monde**	Third World

USEFUL PHRASES

mon pays natal my native country
la capitale de la France the capital of France
de quel pays venez-vous? what country do you come from?
je viens des États-Unis/du Canada I come from the United States/
from Canada
je suis né(e) en Écosse I was born in Scotland
je vais aux Pays-Bas I'm going to the Netherlands
je reviens des États-Unis I have just come back from the United States
les pays en voie de développement the developing countries

ESSENTIAL WORDS (*feminine*)

l'Allemagne	Germany
l'Angleterre	England
la Belgique	Belgium
l'Écosse	Scotland
l'Espagne	Spain
l'Europe	Europe
la France	France
la Grande-Bretagne	Great Britain
la :Hollande	Holland
l'Irlande (du Nord)	(Northern) Ireland
l'Italie	Italy
la Suisse	Switzerland

USEFUL WORDS (*feminine*)

l'Afrique	Africa
l'Algérie	Algeria
l'Amérique	America
l'Amérique du Sud	South America
les Antilles	West Indies
l'Asie	Asia
l'Australie	Australia
l'Autriche	Austria
la Chine	China
la Finlande	Finland
la Grèce	Greece
l'Inde	India
la Norvège	Norway
la Nouvelle-Zélande	New Zealand
la Pologne	Poland
la Roumanie	Romania
la Russie	Russia
la Suède	Sweden
la Tunisie	Tunisia
l'Union européenne, l'UE	European Union, EU

NATIONALITIES

ESSENTIAL WORDS (*masculine*)

un	**Allemand**	a German
un	**Américain**	an American
un	**Anglais**	an Englishman
un	**Belge**	a Belgian
un	**Britannique**	a Briton
un	**Canadien**	a Canadian
un	**Écossais**	a Scot
un	**Espagnol**	a Spaniard
un	**Européen**	a European
un	**Français**	a Frenchman
un	**Gallois**	a Welshman
un	**:Hollandais**	a Dutchman
un	**Irlandais**	an Irishman
un	**Italien**	an Italian
un	**Pakistanais**	a Pakistani
un	**Suisse**	a Swiss

USEFUL PHRASES

il est irlandais, c'est un Irlandais he is Irish
elle est irlandaise, c'est une Irlandaise she is Irish
le paysage irlandais the Irish countryside
une ville irlandaise an Irish town
un Canadien français a French Canadian

ESSENTIAL WORDS *(feminine)*

une	**Allemande**	a German
une	**Américaine**	an American
une	**Anglaise**	an Englishwoman, an English girl
une	**Belge**	a Belgian
une	**Britannique**	a Briton, a British girl *or* woman
une	**Canadienne**	a Canadian
une	**Écossaise**	a Scot
une	**Espagnole**	a Spaniard
une	**Européenne**	a European
une	**Française**	a Frenchwoman, a French girl
une	**Galloise**	a Welshwoman, a Welsh girl
une	**:Hollandaise**	a Dutchwoman, a Dutch girl
une	**Irlandaise**	an Irishwoman, an Irish girl
une	**Italienne**	an Italian
une	**Pakistanaise**	a Pakistani
une	**Suisse**	a Swiss girl *or* woman

USEFUL PHRASES

je suis écossais – je parle anglais I am Scottish – I speak English
une Canadienne française a French Canadian
je suis écossaise I am Scottish
un étranger (une étrangère) a foreigner
à l'étranger abroad; **la nationalité** nationality

USEFUL WORDS (*masculine*)

un	**Africain**	an African
un	**Algérien**	an Algerian
un	**Antillais**	a West Indian
un	**Arabe**	an Arab
un	**Asiatique**	an Asian
un	**Australien**	an Australian
un	**Chinois**	a Chinese
un	**Danois**	a Dane
un	**Finlandais**	a Finn
un	**Grec**	a Greek
un	**Indien**	an Indian
un	**Japonais**	a Japanese
un	**Marocain**	a Moroccan
un	**Néo-Zélandais** (*pl inv*)	a New-Zealander
un	**Polonais**	a Pole
un	**Russe**	a Russian
un	**Tchèque**	a Czech
un	**Tunisien**	a Tunisian

USEFUL WORDS *(feminine)*

une	**Africaine**	an African
une	**Algérienne**	an Algerian
une	**Antillaise**	a West Indian
une	**Arabe**	an Arab
une	**Asiatique**	an Asian
une	**Australienne**	an Australian
une	**Chinoise**	a Chinese
une	**Danoise**	a Dane
une	**Finlandaise**	a Finn
une	**Grecque**	a Greek
une	**Indienne**	an Indian
une	**Japonaise**	a Japanese
une	**Marocaine**	a Moroccan
une	**Néo-Zélandaise** *(pl ~s)*	a New-Zealander
une	**Polonaise**	a Pole
une	**Russe**	a Russian
une	**Tchèque**	a Czech
une	**Tunisienne**	a Tunisian

ESSENTIAL WORDS (*masculine*)

	l'air	air
un	arbre	tree
le	bois	wood
le	bruit	noise
le	champ	field
le	chasseur	hunter
le	château (*pl* -x)	castle
le	chemin	path, way
le	fermier	farmer
le	marché	market
le	pays	country; district
le	paysan	countryman, farmer
le	paysage	scenery
le	pique-nique (*pl* ~s)	picnic
le	pont	bridge
le	ruisseau	stream
le	sentier	track
le	terrain	ground
le	touriste	tourist
le	village	village

USEFUL PHRASES

en plein air in the open air

je connais le chemin du village I know the way to the village

faire un tour en bicyclette to go cycling

les gens du pays the locals

nous avons fait un pique-nique we went for a picnic

ESSENTIAL WORDS *(feminine)*

une	**auberge de jeunesse**	youth hostel
la	**barrière**	gate; fence
la	**camionnette**	van
la	**campagne**	country
la	**canne**	walking stick
la	**ferme**	farm, farmhouse
la	**forêt**	forest
la	**montagne**	mountain
la	**pierre**	stone, rock
la	**promenade**	walk
la	**randonnée**	hike
la	**rivière**	river
la	**route**	road
la	**terre**	earth, ground
la	**tour**	tower
la	**touriste**	tourist
la	**vallée**	valley

USEFUL PHRASES

à la campagne in the country
aller à la campagne to go into the country
habiter à la campagne/en ville to live in the country/in town
cultiver la terre to cultivate the land

IMPORTANT WORDS (*masculine*)

un	**agriculteur**	farmer
les	**campagnards**	country people
le	**fleuve**	river
le	**gendarme** (*m+f*)	policeman
le	**lac**	lake
le	**sommet**	top (*of hill*)

USEFUL WORDS (*masculine*)

le	**bâton**	stick
le	**blé**	corn; wheat
le	**buisson**	bush
le	**caillou** (*pl* -x)	pebble
un	**étang**	pond
le	**foin**	hay
le	**fossé**	ditch
le	**:hameau** (*pl* -x)	hamlet
le	**marais**	marsh
le	**moulin (à vent)**	(wind)mill
le	**poteau** (*pl* -x) **indicateur**	signpost
le	**poteau** (*pl* -x) **télégraphique**	telegraph pole
le	**pré**	meadow
le	**sentier**	path

USEFUL PHRASES
agricole agricultural
paisible, tranquille peaceful
au sommet de la colline at the top of the hill

IMPORTANT WORDS *(feminine)*

l'**agriculture**	agriculture
une **agricultrice**	farmer
une **auberge**	inn
la **botte (de caoutchouc)**	(wellington) boot
la **chaussée**	road surface
la **colline**	hill
la **feuille**	leaf
la **paysanne**	countrywoman
la **poussière**	dust
la **propriété**	property, estate
la **tranquillité**	peace

USEFUL WORDS *(feminine)*

la **boue**	mud
la **bruyère**	heather
la **carrière**	quarry
la **caverne**	cave
la **chasse**	hunting; shooting
la **chute d'eau**	waterfall
la **:haie**	hedge
les **jumelles**	binoculars
la **lande**	moor
la **mare**	pond
la **moisson**	harvest
la **plaine**	plain
la **récolte**	crop, harvest
la **rive**	bank (of river)
les **ruines**	ruins
la **source**	spring, source
les **vendanges**	grape harvest

USEFUL PHRASES

s'égarer, se perdre to lose one's way
faire la moisson to bring in the harvest
faire les vendanges to harvest the grapes

ESSENTIAL WORDS *(masculine)*

l'âge	age
un **air**	appearance
les **cheveux**	hair
les **yeux**	eyes

USEFUL PHRASES

affreux(euse) hideous
agité(e) agitated
aimable nice
amusant(e) amusing, entertaining
barbu(e) bearded, with a beard
beau handsome; **belle** beautiful
bête stupid
calme calm
chauve bald
court(e) short
dégoûtant(e) disgusting
désagréable unpleasant
drôle funny
dynamique dynamic
formidable great
gai(e) cheerful
gentil(le) kind
grand(e) tall
gros(se) fat
heureux(euse) happy
impoli(e) rude
intelligent(e) intelligent
jeune young
joli(e) pretty
laid(e) ugly
long(ue) long
maigre skinny
malheureux(euse) unhappy, unfortunate
méchant(e) naughty
mignon(ne) cute

ESSENTIAL WORDS *(feminine)*

la	**barbe**	beard
la	**couleur**	colour
les	**lentilles (de contact)**	(contact) lenses
les	**lunettes**	glasses
la	**moustache**	moustache
la	**personne**	person
la	**pièce d'identité**	ID
la	**taille**	height, size; waist

USEFUL PHRASES

mince slim

nerveux(euse) nervous, tense

optimiste/pessimiste optimistic/pessimistic

petit(e) small, little

poli polite

sage well-behaved

sérieux(euse) serious

timide shy

vieux, vieille old

elle a l'air triste she looks sad

il pleurait he was crying

il souriait he was smiling

il avait les larmes aux yeux he had tears in his eyes

un homme de taille moyenne a man of average height

je mesure/je fais 1 mètre 70 I am 1 metre 70 tall

de quelle couleur sont tes yeux/tes cheveux? what colour are your eyes/ is your hair?

j'ai les cheveux blonds I have fair hair

j'ai les yeux bleus/verts I have blue eyes/green eyes

les cheveux bruns dark or brown hair

les cheveux châtains chestnut-coloured hair

les cheveux frisés curly hair

les cheveux roux/noirs/blancs red/black/grey hair

les cheveux teints dyed hair

IMPORTANT WORDS (masculine)

le **bouton**	spot
le **caractère**	character, nature
le **regard**	look
le **sourire**	smile
le **teint**	complexion

USEFUL WORDS (masculine)

le **défaut**	fault
le **dentier**	false teeth
le **géant**	giant
le **geste**	gesture
le **grain de beauté**	mole, beauty spot
le **poids**	weight

USEFUL PHRASES

il a bon caractère he is good-tempered
il a mauvais caractère he is bad-tempered
avoir le teint pâle to have a pale complexion
porter des lunettes/des lentilles to wear glasses/contact lenses

IMPORTANT WORDS *(feminine)*

la	**beauté**	beauty
la	**curiosité**	curiosity
une	**expression**	expression
une	**habitude**	habit
	l'**humeur**	mood
la	**laideur**	ugliness
la	**qualité**	(good) quality
la	**voix**	voice

USEFUL WORDS *(feminine)*

la	**boucle**	curl
la	**cicatrice**	scar
les	**fossettes**	dimples
la	**frange**	fringe
la	**permanente**	perm
la	**ressemblance**	resemblance
les	**rides**	wrinkles
les	**taches de rousseur**	freckles
la	**timidité**	shyness

USEFUL PHRASES

je suis toujours de bonne humeur I am always in a good mood
il est de mauvaise humeur he is in a bad mood
il s'est mis en colère he got angry
elle ressemble à sa mère she looks like her mother
il se ronge les ongles he bites his nails

ESSENTIAL WORDS (*masculine*)

	l'allemand	German
	l'alphabet	alphabet
	l'anglais	English
	l'apprentissage	apprenticeship; learning
le	cahier de texte(s)	homework book
le	camarade de classe	school friend
le	carnet	notebook
le	club	club
le	collège	secondary school
le	copain	pal
les	cours	lessons
le	crayon	pencil
le	dessin	drawing
le	devoir	test
les	devoirs	homework
le	directeur	headmaster
le	dortoir	dormitory
un	échange	exchange
un	écolier	schoolboy
un	élève	pupil, schoolboy
un	emploi du temps	timetable
	l'enseignement	education, teaching
	l'espagnol	Spanish
un	étudiant	student
un	examen	exam
un	examen blanc	mock exam
un	exposé	presentation
le	français	French
le	groupe	group
le	gymnase	gym(nasium)
	l'italien	Italian
le	laboratoire	laboratory
le	livre	book
le	lycée	secondary school

ESSENTIAL WORDS (*feminine*)

la	**biologie**	biology
la	**camarade de classe**	school friend
la	**cantine**	dining hall, canteen
la	**carte**	map
la	**chimie**	chemistry
la	**classe**	class; year; classroom
la	**copine**	pal
la	**directrice**	headmistress
une	**école**	school
une	**école maternelle**	nursery school
une	**école primaire**	primary school
une	**écolière**	schoolgirl
	l'**éducation physique**	PE
	l'**électronique**	electronics
une	**élève**	pupil, schoolgirl
	l'**EPS**	PE
une	**erreur**	mistake
	l'**étude (de)**	study (of)
les	**études**	studies
une	**étudiante**	student
une	**excursion**	trip, outing
une	**expérience**	experiment
la	**faute**	mistake
la	**géographie**	geography
la	**gomme**	rubber
les	**grandes vacances**	summer holidays
la	**gymnastique**	gym(nastics)
	l'**histoire**	history; story
	l'**informatique**	computer studies
la	**journée**	day
les	**langues (vivantes)**	(modern) languages
la	**leçon**	lesson
la	**lecture**	reading
les	**mathématiques**	mathematics
les	**maths**	maths
la	**matière**	(school) subject
la	**musique**	music

ESSENTIAL WORDS (*masculine continued*)

le	**mot**	word
un	**ordinateur**	computer
le	**prix**	prize
le	**professeur**	teacher
le	**professeur des écoles**	primary schoolteacher
les	**progrès**	progress
le	**résultat**	result
le	**self**	cafeteria
le	**semestre**	semester
le	**stylo**	pen
le	**tableau (noir)**	blackboard
le	**travail**	work
les	**travaux manuels**	handicrafts
les	**travaux pratiques**	practical class
le	**trimestre**	term

USEFUL PHRASES

travailler to work
apprendre to learn
étudier to study
depuis combien de temps apprenez-vous le français? how long have you been learning French?
apprendre qch par cœur to learn sth off by heart
j'ai des devoirs tous les jours I have homework every day
ma petite sœur va à l'école – moi, je vais au collège my little sister goes to primary school – I go to secondary school
enseigner le français to teach French
le professeur d'allemand the German teacher
j'ai fait des progrès en maths I have made progress in maths
passer un examen to sit an exam
être reçu(e) à un examen to pass an exam
échouer à un examen to fail an exam
avoir la moyenne to get a pass mark

ESSENTIAL WORDS *(feminine continued)*

la	**natation**	swimming
la	**note**	mark
la	**phrase**	sentence
la	**physique**	physics
la	**piscine**	swimming pool
la	**professeur**	teacher
la	**professeur des écoles**	primary schoolteacher
la	**question**	question
la	**récréation**	break
la	**rentrée (des classes)**	beginning of term
la	**réponse**	answer
la	**salle de classe**	classroom
la	**salle des professeurs**	staffroom
les	**sciences**	science
une	**université**	university
les	**vacances**	holidays

USEFUL PHRASES

facile/difficile easy/difficult
intéressant(e) interesting
ennuyeux(euse) boring
lire to read; **écrire** to write
écouter to listen (to)
regarder to look at, watch
répéter to repeat
répondre to reply
parler to speak
elle est première/dernière de la classe she is top/bottom of the class
entrer en classe to go into the classroom
faire une erreur to make a mistake
corriger to correct
j'ai fait une faute de grammaire I made a grammatical mistake
j'ai eu une bonne note I got a good mark
répondez à la question! answer the question!

IMPORTANT WORDS *(masculine)*

le	**baccalauréat, le bac**	French school-leaving certificate/exam
le	**bulletin**	report
le	**bureau**	office
le	**certificat**	certificate
le	**classeur**	folder, file
le	**concours**	competitive exam
le	**conseil de classe**	staff meeting (*to discuss progress of pupils*)
le	**couloir**	corridor
le	**cours magistral**	lecture
le	**diplôme**	diploma
le	**dossier**	file
un	**écrit**	written exam
un	**instituteur**	primary schoolteacher
le	**livre électronique**	e-book
un	**oral**	oral exam
le	**papier**	paper
le	**règlement**	rules

USEFUL PHRASES

mon ami prépare son bac my friend is sitting his school-leaving exam
  (*like A-levels*)
les Français n'ont pas classe le mercredi après-midi French children have
  Wednesday afternoons off
réviser ses leçons to revise
je vais réviser la leçon demain I'll go over the lesson again tomorrow

IMPORTANT WORDS (*feminine*)

une	**absence**	absence
une	**appréciation**	comment (*from teacher*)
la	**conférence**	lecture
la	**cour (de récréation)**	playground
une	**institutrice**	primary schoolteacher
les	**langues anciennes**	ancient languages
une	**LV1 (langue vivante 1)**	first foreign language studied
une	**LV2 (langue vivante 2)**	second foreign language studied
la	**mention**	grade
la	**règle**	rule; ruler
la	**traduction**	translation
la	**trousse**	pencil case
la	**version**	translation (from foreign language)

USEFUL PHRASES

en sixième in Year 7, in the first form
en cinquième in Year 8, in the second form
en quatrième in Year 9, in the third form
en troisième in Year 10, in the fourth form
en seconde in Year 11, in the fifth form
en première in lower sixth
en terminale in upper sixth

présent(e) present
absent(e) absent
punir un élève to punish a pupil
mettre une colle à qn to give sb detention
taisez-vous! be quiet!
levez la main! put your hand up!

USEFUL WORDS *(masculine)*

le	**Bic®**	Biro®
le	**brouillon**	rough copy
le	**cahier**	exercise book, jotter
le	**calcul**	sum
le	**cartable**	satchel
le	**collège technique**	technical college
le	**correcteur (liquide)**	correction fluid
le	**dictionnaire**	dictionary
un	**examinateur**	examiner
un	**exercice**	exercise
le	**feutre**	felt-tip pen
le	**grec**	Greek
un	**inspecteur**	school inspector
un	**internat**	boarding school
le	**latin**	Latin
le	**lycéen**	secondary school pupil
le	**lycée professionnel**	vocational school
le	**manuel**	textbook
le	**pensionnaire**	boarder
le	**principal**	headmaster *(of collège)*
le	**professeur principal**	form tutor
le	**proviseur**	headmaster *(of lycée)*
le	**pupitre**	desk
le	**rang**	row *(of seats etc)*
le	**russe**	Russian
le	**sac à dos**	backpack
le	**stylo bille**	Biro®
le	**stylo feutre**	felt-tip pen
le	**surveillant**	supervisor
le	**tableau interactif**	interactive whiteboard
le	**taille-crayon** *(pl ~s)*	pencil sharpener
le	**test**	test
le	**thème**	prose translation
le	**trimestre**	term
le	**vestiaire**	cloakroom
le	**vocabulaire**	vocabulary

USEFUL WORDS (*feminine*)

l'**algèbre**	algebra
l'**arithmétique**	arithmetic
la **calculatrice**, la **calculette**	calculator
la **colle**	detention; difficult question
la **composition**	essay; class exam
la **conduite**	behaviour
la **craie**	chalk
la **distribution des prix**	prize-giving
une **école maternelle**	nursery school
une **école normale**	College of Education
l'**écriture**	handwriting
l'**éducation civique**	civics
l'**encre**	ink
une **épreuve**	test
la **faculté**, la **fac**	university; faculty
la **feuille de présence**	absence sheet
la **géométrie**	geometry
la **grammaire**	grammar
une **inspectrice**	school inspector
la **lycéenne**	secondary school pupil
la **moyenne**	pass mark; average mark
l'**orthographe**	spelling
la **poésie**	poetry, poem
la **punition**	punishment
la **retenue**	detention
la **sacoche**	schoolbag, satchel
les **SVT (sciences de la vie et de la terre)**	environmental science
la **serviette**	briefcase
la **surveillante**	supervisor
la **tache**	blot
la **tâche**	task
la **technologie**	technology
les **TIC (technologies de l'information et de la communication)**	ICT

ESSENTIAL WORDS (*masculine*)

	l'air	air
les	animaux	animals
les	arbres	trees
le	bois	wood
un	écologiste	environmentalist
	l'environnement	environment
les	fruits	fruit
le	gas-oil	diesel
le	gaz	gas
les	gaz à effet de serre	greenhouse gases
les	gaz d'échappement	exhaust fumes
les	habitants	inhabitants
les	légumes	vegetables
le	monde	world
le	pays	country
les	poissons	fish
le	temps	weather; time
les	Verts	the Greens
le	verre	glass

IMPORTANT WORDS (*masculine*)

	l'aluminium	aluminium
	l'avenir	future
le	biocarburant	biofuel
le	changement climatique	climate change
le	climat	climate
le(s)	dégât(s)	damage
le	détergent	detergent
le	développement durable	sustainable development
le	fleuve	river
le	gouvernement	government
le	lac	lake
le	parc éolien	wind farm
le	polluant	pollutant
le	trou dans la couche d'ozone	hole in the ozone layer

ESSENTIAL WORDS (feminine)

les	**bouteilles**	bottles
la	**carte**	map
la	**côte**	coast
	l'**eau**	water
	l'**écologie**	ecology
	l'**empreinte carbone**	carbon footprint
une	**éolienne**	wind turbine
une	**espèce**	species
	l'**essence**	petrol
les	**fleurs**	flowers
une	**île**	island
la	**mer**	sea
la	**montagne**	mountain
la	**plage**	beach
les	**plantes**	plants
la	**pluie**	rain
la	**pollution**	pollution
la	**question**	question
la	**région**	region, area
la	**rivière**	river
la	**température**	temperature
la	**terre**	earth
une	**usine**	factory
la	**voiture**	car

IMPORTANT WORDS (feminine)

la	**centrale nucléaire**	nuclear plant
la	**chaleur**	heat
la	**crise**	crisis
la	**forêt**	forest
la	**lessive**	washing powder; washing
la	**planète**	planet
la	**solution**	solution
la	**taxe**	tax
la	**zone**	zone

USEFUL WORDS (*masculine*)

les	**aliments bio**	organic food
un	**aérosol**	aerosol
le	**canal** (*pl* canaux)	canal
les	**CFC**	CFC
le	**chercheur**	researcher
le	**combustible**	fuel
le	**commerce équitable**	fair trade
le	**continent**	continent
les	**déchets nucléaires/ industriels**	nuclear/industrial waste
le	**dépotoir**	dumping ground
le	**désert**	desert
le	**développement durable**	sustainable development
un	**écosystème**	ecosystem
un	**engrais (chimique)**	(artificial) fertilizer
un	**océan**	ocean
les	**OGM**	GMO
le	**panneau solaire** (*pl* ~x ~s)	solar panel
le	**pot catalytique**	catalytic converter
le	**produit**	product
les	**produits chimiques**	chemicals
le	**réchauffement planétaire**	global warming
le	**recyclage**	recycling
les	**scientifiques**	scientists
	l'**univers**	universe

USEFUL PHRASES

il est très écolo he's very environmentally-minded
un produit écologique an eco-friendly product
à l'avenir in the future
polluer to pollute; **détruire** to destroy
contaminer to contaminate
interdire to ban
sauver to save
recycler to recycle
hybride hybrid
vert(e) green

USEFUL WORDS *(feminine)*

la	**biodiversité**	biodiversity
la	**catastrophe**	disaster
	l'**énergie éolienne**	wind power
	l'**énergie nucléaire**	nuclear power
une	**énergie renouvelable**	renewable energy
	l'**énergie solaire**	solar energy
une	**éruption**	eruption
la	**forêt tropicale humide**	tropical rainforest
la	**lune**	moon
la	**marée noire**	oil slick
la	**nocivité**	harmfulness
les	**pluies acides**	acid rain
la	**pollution sonore**	noise pollution
la	**population**	population
les	**vidanges**	sewage
la	**voiture électrique/hybride**	electric/hybrid car

USEFUL PHRASES

biodégradable biodegradable

nocif(ive) pour l'environnement harmful to the environment

biologique organic

l'essence sans plomb unleaded petrol

les espèces en voie de disparition endangered species

ESSENTIAL WORDS (*masculine*)

les	**adultes**	adults
l'	**âge**	age
le	**bébé**	baby
le	**cousin**	cousin
un	**enfant**	child
le	**fiancé**	fiancé
le	**fils** [fis]	son
le	**frère**	brother
le	**garçon**	boy
les	**gens**	people
le	**grand-père** (*pl* ~s~s)	grandfather
les	**grands-parents**	grandparents
un	**homme**	man
le	**jeune homme**	youth, young man
les	**jeunes**	young people
le	**mari**	husband
le	**nom**	name
le	**nom de famille**	surname
le	**nom de jeune fille**	maiden name
un	**oncle**	uncle
le	**papa**	daddy
le	**parent**	relative
les	**parents**	parents
le	**père**	father
le	**prénom**	first *or* Christian name

USEFUL PHRASES

quel âge avez-vous? how old are you?
j'ai 15 ans – il a 40 ans I'm 15 – he is 40
comment vous appelez-vous? what is your name?
je m'appelle Robert my name is Robert
il s'appelle Jean-Pierre his name is Jean-Pierre
fiancé(e) engaged
marié(e) married
divorcé(e) divorced
séparé(e) separated
épouser qn, se marier avec qn to marry sb
se marier to get married; **divorcer** to get divorced

ESSENTIAL WORDS (feminine)

la	**cousine**	cousin
une	**enfant**	child
la	**famille**	family
la	**femme**	woman; wife
la	**fiancée**	fiancée
la	**fille**	daughter; girl
la	**grand-mère** (pl ~s~s)	grandmother
les	**grandes personnes**	grown-ups
la	**maman**	mummy
la	**mère**	mother
la	**sœur**	sister
la	**tante**	aunt

USEFUL PHRASES

plus jeune/âgé que moi younger/older than me
as-tu des frères et sœurs? do you have any brothers or sisters?
j'ai un frère et une sœur I have one brother and one sister
je n'ai pas de frères/de sœurs I don't have any brothers/sisters
je suis enfant unique I am an only child
toute la famille the whole family
grandir to grow
vieillir to get old
je m'entends bien avec mes parents I get on well with my parents
ma mère travaille my mother works

IMPORTANT WORDS (*masculine*)

un	**ado(lescent)**	teenager
un	**arrière-grand-père** (*pl* ~s~s)	great-grandfather
les	**arrière-grands-parents**	great-grandparents
le	**beau-père** (*pl* ~x~s)	father-in-law; stepfather
le	**célibataire**	bachelor
le	**compagnon**	partner
	l'époux	husband
le	**mariage**	marriage; wedding
le	**neveu**	nephew
le	**PACS**	civil partnership
le	**petit-fils** [pətifis] (*pl* ~s~)	grandson
les	**petits-enfants** [pətizãfã]	grandchildren
le	**veuf**	widower

USEFUL WORDS (*masculine*)

le	**beau-fils** [bofis] (*pl* ~x~)	son-in-law; stepson
le	**beau-frère** (*pl* ~x~s)	brother-in-law
le	**couple**	couple
le	**demi-frère** (*pl* ~s)	stepbrother
le	**filleul**	godson
le	**gendre**	son-in-law
le	**gosse**	kid
les	**jumeaux**	twins
le	**marié**	bridegroom
les	**nouveaux mariés**	newly-weds
un	**orphelin**	orphan
le	**parrain**	godfather
le	**retraité**	pensioner
le	**surnom**	nickname
les	**triplés**	triplets
le	**vieillard**	old man

USEFUL PHRASES

naître to be born
vivre to live
mourir to die
je suis né(e) en 2001 I was born in 2001
ma grand-mère est morte my grandmother is dead
elle est morte en 1995 she died in 1995

IMPORTANT WORDS (feminine)

une **ado(lescente)**	teenager
les **allocations familiales**	child benefit
une **arrière-grand-mère** (pl ~s~s)	great-grandmother
la **belle-mère** (pl ~s~s)	mother-in-law; stepmother
la **célibataire**	single woman
la **compagne**	partner
une **épouse**	wife
la **jeune fille au pair**	au pair girl
la **jeunesse**	youth
la **nièce**	niece
la **petite-fille** (pl ~s~s)	granddaughter
la **veuve**	widow

USEFUL WORDS (feminine)

la **belle-fille** (pl ~s~s)	daughter-in-law; stepdaughter
la **belle-sœur** (pl ~s~s)	sister-in-law
la **demi-sœur** (pl ~s)	stepsister
la **famille monoparentale**	single-parent family
la **femme au foyer**	housewife
la **filleule**	goddaughter
la **gosse**	kid
la **jeune mariée**	bride
les **jumelles**	twins, twin sisters
la **marraine**	godmother
la **nurse**	nanny
une **orpheline**	orphan
la **retraitée**	pensioner
la **vieillesse**	old age

USEFUL PHRASES

il/elle est célibataire he/she is single
il est veuf he is a widower
elle est veuve she is a widow
je suis le cadet (la cadette) I am the youngest
je suis l'aîné(e) I am the eldest
ma sœur aînée my older sister
mon petit frère my little brother

ESSENTIAL WORDS (*masculine*)

un **agriculteur**	farmer
un **animal** (*pl* animaux)	animal
le **bœuf** [bœf] (*pl* -s [bø])	ox
le **canard**	duck
le **champ**	field
le **chat**	cat
le **cheval** (*pl* chevaux)	horse
le **chien**	dog
le **chien de berger**	sheepdog
le **cochon**	pig
le **dindon**	turkey
le **fermier**	farmer
le **mouton**	sheep
le **poulet**	chicken
le **veau** (*pl* -x)	calf
le **village**	village

IMPORTANT WORDS (*masculine*)

un **agneau** (*pl* -x)	lamb
le **coq**	cock
le **paysan**	countryman
le **tracteur**	tractor

USEFUL PHRASES

l'agriculture **biologique** organic farming
l'agriculture **intensive** intensive farming
un champ de **blé** a cornfield
l'**élevage en batterie** battery farming
s'occuper des animaux to look after the animals
traire les vaches to milk the cows
rentrer la moisson to bring in the harvest

ESSENTIAL WORDS (feminine)

une	**agricultrice**	farmer
la	**barrière**	gate; fence
la	**brebis**	ewe
la	**camionnette**	van
la	**campagne**	country
une	**exploitation agricole**	farm
la	**ferme**	farm; farmhouse
la	**fermière**	farmer; farmer's wife
la	**forêt**	forest
la	**jument**	mare
la	**poule**	hen
la	**serre**	greenhouse
la	**terre**	earth, ground
la	**truie**	sow
la	**vache**	cow

IMPORTANT WORDS (feminine)

la	**colline**	hill
la	**paysanne**	countrywoman

USEFUL PHRASES

vivre à la campagne to live in the country
travailler dans une ferme to work on a farm
faire la récolte to bring in the crops
faire les foins to make hay
les poulets élevés en plein air free range chickens
les œufs de poules élevées en plein air free range eggs

USEFUL WORDS (*masculine*)

un	âne	donkey
le	bélier	ram
le	berger	shepherd
le	bétail	cattle
le	blé	corn; wheat
le	chevreau (*pl* -x)	kid
un	élevage	cattle farm
un	engrais	fertilizer
un	épouvantail	scarecrow
un	étang	pond
le	foin	hay
le	fossé	ditch
le	fumier	manure
le	grain	grain, seed
le	grenier	loft
le	:hangar	shed, barn
le	maïs [mais]	maize
le	marché	market
le	moulin (à vent)	(wind)mill
le	paysage	landscape
le	porc [pɔR]	pig
le	poulailler	henhouse
le	poulain	foal
le	poussin	chick
le	pré	meadow
le	puits	well
le	raisin	grape
le	seigle	rye
le	sillon	furrow
le	silo	silo
le	sol	ground, earth
le	taureau (*pl* -x)	bull
le	troupeau (*pl* -x)	(*sheep*) flock; (*cattle*) herd

USEFUL WORDS (*feminine*)

	l'avoine	oats
la	basse-cour (*pl* ~s~s)	farmyard
la	boue	mud
la	céréale	cereal crop
la	charrette	cart
la	charrue	plough
la	chaumière	(thatched) cottage
la	chèvre	goat
une	échelle	ladder
une	écurie	stable
une	étable	cow-shed, byre
la	foire	fair
la	grange	barn
la	laine	wool
la	lande	moor, heath
la	meule de foin	haystack
la	moisson	harvest
la	moissonneuse-batteuse	combine harvester
	(*pl* ~s~s)	
une	oie	goose
	l'orge	barley
la	paille	straw
la	porcherie	pigsty
la	récolte	crop
les	vendanges	grape harvest, grape picking
la	vigne	vine

ESSENTIAL WORDS (*masculine*)

les	**fruits de mer**	seafood
le	**poisson**	fish
le	**poisson rouge**	goldfish

IMPORTANT WORDS (*masculine*)

le	**crabe**	crab
un	**insecte**	insect

USEFUL WORDS (*masculine*)

un	**aquarium**	aquarium
le	**brochet**	pike
le	**cafard**	cockroach
le	**calmar**	squid
le	**criquet**	cricket
le	**frelon**	hornet
le	**grillon**	cricket
le	**:haddock**	haddock
le	**:hareng**	herring
le	**:homard**	lobster
le	**merlan**	whiting
le	**moucheron**	midge
le	**moustique**	mosquito
le	**papillon**	butterfly
le	**papillon de nuit**	moth
le	**poulpe**	octopus
le	**requin**	shark
le	**saumon**	salmon
le	**têtard**	tadpole
le	**thon**	tuna
le	**ver**	worm
le	**ver à soie**	silkworm

USEFUL PHRASES

nager to swim
voler to fly
nous allons à la pêche we're going fishing

ESSENTIAL WORDS (*feminine*)

l'eau water

IMPORTANT WORDS (*feminine*)

la **mouche** fly
la **sardine** sardine
la **truite** trout

USEFUL WORDS (*feminine*)

une **abeille** bee
une **aile** wing
une **anguille** eel
une **araignée** spider
la **chenille** caterpillar
la **cigale** cicada
la **coccinelle** [kɔksinɛl] ladybird
la **crevette** shrimp
la **fourmi** ant
la **grenouille** frog
la **guêpe** wasp
une **huître** oyster
la **langouste** crayfish
les **langoustines** scampi
la **libellule** dragonfly
la **limande** dab
la **méduse** jellyfish
la **morue** (salt) cod
la **moule** mussel
la **pieuvre** octopus
la **puce** flea
la **punaise** bug
la **sauterelle** grasshopper
la **sole** sole

USEFUL PHRASES
une **piqûre** de **guêpe** a wasp sting
une **toile** d'**araignée** a spider's web

ESSENTIAL WORDS (*masculine*)

	l'**alcool**	alcohol
un	**apéritif**	aperitif
le	**bar**	bar
le	**beurre**	butter
le	**bifteck**	steak
le	**bœuf**	beef
le	**bol**	bowl
les	**bonbons**	sweets
le	**café**	coffee; café
le	**café au lait**	milky coffee
le	**café-crème**	coffee with milk
le	**chocolat (chaud)**	(hot) chocolate
le	**cidre**	cider
le	**coca**	Coke®
le	**couteau** (*pl* -x)	knife
le	**croissant**	croissant
le	**croque-monsieur** (*pl inv*)	ham and cheese toastie
le	**cuisinier**	cook
le	**déjeuner**	lunch
le	**demi**	half-pint
le	**dessert**	dessert
le	**dîner**	dinner
le	**fromage**	cheese
un	**fruit**	piece of fruit
les	**fruits**	fruit
les	**fruits de mer**	seafood
le	**garçon (de café)**	waiter
le	**gâteau** (*pl* -x)	cake
le	**:hamburger**	hamburger
les	**:hors-d'œuvre**	hors d'œuvre, starters
le	**jambon**	ham
le	**jus de fruit**	fruit juice
le	**lait**	milk
les	**légumes**	vegetables
le	**menu**	fixed-price menu
un	**œuf** [œf] (*pl* -s [ø])	egg

ESSENTIAL WORDS *(feminine)*

	l'addition	bill
une	assiette	plate
la	baguette	French loaf
la	bière	beer
la	boisson	drink
la	boîte	tin, can; box
la	bouteille	bottle
la	carte	menu
les	céréales	cereal
la	confiture	jam
la	confiture d'oranges	marmalade
la	conserve	canned food
la	crêpe	pancake
les	crudités	mixed raw vegetables
la	cuiller, la cuillère	spoon
	l'eau (minérale)	(mineral) water
une	entrecôte	(entrecôte) steak
une	entrée	first course
la	faim	hunger
la	fourchette	fork
les	frites	chips
la	glace	ice cream
	l'huile	oil
la	limonade	lemonade
une	olive	olive
une	omelette	omelette
la	pâtisserie	pastry; patisserie
la	poissonnerie	fish shop
les	pommes frites	chips
la	quiche	quiche
la	salade	salad
la	saucisse	sausage
la	soif	thirst
la	soucoupe	saucer
la	soupe	soup
la	table	table
la	tasse	cup

ESSENTIAL WORDS (*masculine continued*)

un **œuf à la coque**	soft-boiled egg
un **œuf dur**	hard-boiled egg
le **pain**	bread
le **pain grillé**	toast
le **pain au chocolat**	pain au chocolat
le **pâté**	pâté
le **patron**	owner
le **petit déjeuner**	breakfast
le **pique-nique** (*pl* ~s)	picnic
le **plat**	dish; course
le **plat du jour**	today's special
le **plateau** (*pl* ~x)	tray
les **plats cuisinés**	ready-made meals
le **poisson**	fish
le **porc** [pɔʀ]	pork
le **potage**	soup
le **poulet (rôti)**	(roast) chicken
le **quart**	quarter (*bottle/litre etc*)
le **repas**	meal
le **restaurant**	restaurant
le **riz**	rice
le **rôti**	roast
le **sandwich** [sɑ̃dwitʃ]	sandwich
le **saucisson**	salami
le **sel**	salt
le **self**	self-service restaurant
le **service**	service
le **steak** [stɛk]	steak
le **sucre**	sugar
le **thé**	tea
le **veau**	veal
le **verre**	glass
le **vin**	wine
le **vinaigre**	vinegar
le **yaourt**	yoghurt

ESSENTIAL WORDS *(feminine continued)*

la	**tranche (de)**	slice (of)
la	**vaisselle**	dishes
la	**viande**	meat

IMPORTANT WORDS *(feminine)*

la	**brasserie**	restaurant
la	**cafétéria**	cafeteria
la	**carafe**	carafe, jug
les	**chips**	crisps
la	**côte de porc**	pork chop
la	**crème**	cream
la	**cuiller à café/à dessert/**	teaspoon/dessert spoon/
	à soupe	tablespoon
la	**farine**	flour
la	**grillade**	grilled meat
la	**mayonnaise**	mayonnaise
la	**merguez**	spicy sausage
la	**moutarde**	mustard
une	**odeur**	smell
la	**pizza**	pizza
la	**pression**	draught beer
la	**recette**	recipe
la	**serveuse**	waitress
la	**tarte**	tart
la	**terrine**	pâté
la	**théière**	teapot
la	**vanille**	vanilla

IMPORTANT WORDS (*masculine*)

	l'agneau	lamb
	l'ail	garlic
le	chariot	trolley
le	chef (*m+f*)	chef
le	choix	choice
le	commerce équitable	fair trade
le	couvert	cover charge; place setting
les	escargots	snails
le	goût	taste
le	goûter	snack
le	lapin	rabbit
le	mouton	mutton
le	parfum	flavour
le	pichet	jug
le	poivre	pepper
le	pourboire	tip
le	prix fixe	set price
le	prix net	inclusive price
le	serveur	waiter
le	sirop	syrup; cordial
le	supplément	extra charge

USEFUL WORDS (*masculine*)

le	bouchon	cork
le	cacao	cocoa
le	casse-croûte (*pl inv*)	snack
le	champagne	champagne
le	citron pressé	freshly-squeezed lemon juice
le	cognac	brandy
le	foie	liver
le	gibier	game
le	glaçon	ice cube
le	ketchup	ketchup
le	lard	bacon
les	lardons	diced bacon
le	miel	honey
un	ouvre-boîtes (*pl inv*)	tin opener
le	panaché	shandy

USEFUL WORDS (*feminine*)

une	**assiette anglaise**	selection of cold meats
la	**biscotte**	Melba toast
la	**brioche**	bun
la	**carte des vins**	wine list
la	**côtelette**	chop
la	**crème anglaise**	custard
la	**crème Chantilly**	whipped cream
la	**cruche**	jug
les	**cuisses de grenouille**	frogs' legs
la	**gelée**	jelly
une	**infusion**	herbal tea
la	**margarine**	margarine
la	**miette**	crumb
les	**moules**	mussels
la	**nappe**	tablecloth
la	**nourriture**	food
la	**paille**	straw
les	**pâtes**	pasta
la	**purée**	mashed potatoes
les	**rillettes**	potted meat (*made of pork or goose*)
la	**sauce**	sauce; gravy
la	**serviette**	napkin
la	**tartine**	piece of bread and butter
la	**tisane**	herbal tea
les	**tripes**	tripe
la	**vinaigrette**	vinaigrette dressing
la	**volaille**	poultry

USEFUL PHRASES

cuisiner to cook
manger to eat
boire to drink
avaler to swallow
mon plat préféré my favourite dish
qu'est-ce que tu bois? what are you having to drink?
c'est bon it's nice

USEFUL WORDS (*masculine continued*)

le	**petit pain**	roll
le	**ragoût**	stew
les	**rognons**	kidneys
le	**rosbif**	roast beef
le	**thermos**	flask
le	**tire-bouchon** (*pl* ~s)	corkscrew
un	**toast**	slice of toast
le	**whisky**	whisky

USEFUL PHRASES

déjeuner to have lunch

dîner to have dinner

goûter qch to taste sth

ça sent bon! that smells good!

le vin blanc/rosé/rouge white/rosé/red wine

un steak saignant/à point/bien cuit a rare/medium/well-done steak

avoir faim to be hungry

avoir soif to be thirsty

mettre le couvert, mettre la table to set the table

débarrasser to clear the table

faire la vaisselle to do the dishes

nous goûtons en rentrant de l'école we have a snack when we come back from school

prendre le petit déjeuner to have breakfast

délicieux(ieuse) delicious

dégoûtant(e) disgusting

bon appétit! enjoy your meal!

à votre santé! cheers!

l'addition, s'il vous plaît! the bill please!

est-ce que le service est compris? is service included?

"service (non) compris" "service (not) included"

manger au restaurant to eat out

inviter qn à déjeuner to invite sb to lunch

prendre l'apéritif to have drinks

SMOKING

le	**briquet**	lighter
le	**tabac**	tobacco; tobacconist's
le	**cendrier**	ashtray
le	**cigare**	cigar
un	**espace fumeur(s)**	smoking area
le	**timbre à la nicotine**	nicotine patch
une	**allumette**	match
la	**cigarette**	cigarette
la	**cigarette électronique**	e-cigarette
la	**pipe**	pipe
la	**zone fumeur(s)**	smoking area

USEFUL PHRASES

une boîte d'allumettes a box of matches
avez-vous du feu? do you have a light?
allumer une cigarette to light up
"défense de fumer" "no smoking"
je ne fume pas I don't smoke
j'ai arrêté de fumer I've stopped smoking
fumer est très mauvais pour la santé smoking is very bad for you
vapoter to vape, to smoke an e-cigarette

ESSENTIAL WORDS (*masculine*)

un	**appareil-photo** (*pl* ~s~s)	camera
	l'**argent de poche**	pocket money
le	**baby-sitting**	baby-sitting
le	**babyfoot**	table football
le	**baladeur**	personal stereo
le	**billet**	ticket
le	**CD**	CD
le	**chanteur**	singer
le	**cinéma**	cinema
le	**club**	club
le	**concert**	concert
les	**copains**	friends
le	**correspondant**	pen friend
le	**DVD**	DVD
les	**échecs**	chess
le	**film**	film
le	**:hobby**	hobby
	l'**Internet**	internet
le	**jeu** (*pl* -x)	game
le	**jeu vidéo**	video game, computer game
le	**journal** (*pl* journaux)	newspaper
le	**lecteur de CD/DVD/MP3**	CD/DVD/MP3 player
le	**magazine (people)**	(celebrity) magazine
le	**membre**	member
le	**musée**	museum; art gallery
un	**ordinateur**	computer
un	**ordinateur portable**	laptop
le	**passe-temps** (*pl inv*)	hobby
le	**programme**	programme
le	**roman**	novel
le	**roman policier**	detective novel
le	**spectacle**	show
le	**sport**	sports
le	**(téléphone) portable**	mobile (phone)
le	**temps libre**	free time
le	**théâtre**	theatre
le	**week-end** (*pl* ~s)	weekend

ESSENTIAL WORDS (feminine)

la	**bande dessinée**	comic strip
la	**brochure**	leaflet
les	**cartes**	cards
la	**chaîne de télévision**	TV channel
la	**chanson**	song; singing
la	**chanteuse**	singer
la	**console de jeu**	games console
les	**copines**	(girl)friends
la	**correspondante**	pen friend
la	**danse**	dance; dancing
la	**distraction**	entertainment
une	**excursion**	trip, outing
la	**fête**	party
les	**informations**	news
l'	**informatique**	computing
la	**lecture**	reading
la	**musique (pop/classique)**	(pop/classical) music
la	**patinoire**	skating rink
la	**photo**	photo
la	**presse**	the press
la	**promenade**	walk
la	**publicité**	publicity
la	**radio**	radio
la	**revue**	magazine
la	**tablette**	tablet
la	**télé(vision)**	TV, television
la	**vedette (de cinéma)** (m+f)	(film) star

USEFUL PHRASES

je sors avec mes amis I go out with my friends
je lis les journaux, je regarde la télévision I read the newspapers,
  I watch television
bricoler to do DIY
faire du baby-sitting to baby-sit
je joue au football/au tennis/aux cartes I play football/tennis/cards
je joue de la guitare I play the guitar
zapper to channel-hop

IMPORTANT WORDS (*masculine*)

un	**appareil-photo numérique**	digital camera
le	**caméscope**	camcorder
le	**concours**	competition
le	**dessin animé**	cartoon
le	**disque compact**	compact disc, CD
le	**feuilleton**	serial; soap
le	**graveur de CD/DVD**	CD/DVD writer
le	**jouet**	toy
les	**loisirs**	leisure activities
le	**PC**	PC, personal computer
le	**petit ami**	boyfriend
le	**rendez-vous**	date
le	**site web**	website
le	**SMS**, le **texto**	text message
le	**tricot**	knitting

USEFUL WORDS (*masculine*)

le	**blog**	blog
le	**chat** [tʃat]	chat; chatroom
un	**éclaireur**	scout
le	**fan** [fan]	fan
le	**forum**	forum
le	**:hit-parade**	charts
le	**jeu de société**	board game
les	**mots croisés**	crossword puzzle(s)
les	**people**	celebrities
le	**scout**	scout
le	**skate(board)**	skateboard
le	**vidéoclub**	video shop

USEFUL PHRASES

passionnant(e) exciting
ennuyeux(euse) boring
amusant(e) funny
pas mal not bad, quite good
faire des photos, prendre des photos to take photos
je m'ennuie I'm bored

IMPORTANT WORDS *(feminine)*

les	**actualités**	news
une	**affiche**	notice; poster
la	**carte mémoire**	memory card
la	**collection**	collection
une	**émission**	programme
une	**exposition**	exhibition
la	**maison des jeunes**	youth club
la	**peinture**	painting
la	**petite amie**	girlfriend
la	**petite annonce**	advert; small ad
la	**randonnée**	hike
la	**réunion**	meeting
la	**soirée**	evening

USEFUL WORDS *(feminine)*

la	**boîte de nuit**	night club
la	**chorale**	choir
la	**colonie de vacances**	holiday camp
la	**diapositive**	slide
une	**éclaireuse**	girl guide
la	**méchanique**	mechanics
la	**photographie**	photograph; photography
la	**planche de skate**	skateboard

USEFUL PHRASES

aller en boîte to go clubbing

danser to dance

on se réunit le vendredi we meet on Fridays

on se retrouve à vingt heures devant le cinéma see you at 8pm in front of the cinema

j'ai rendez-vous avec elle samedi I have a date with her on Saturday

je fais des économies pour m'acheter un lecteur de mp3 I'm saving up to buy an MP3 player

j'aimerais faire le tour du monde I'd like to go round the world

ESSENTIAL WORDS (*masculine*)

un	**abricot**	apricot
un	**ananas**	pineapple
le	**citron**	lemon
un	**fruit**	piece of fruit
les	**fruits**	fruit
le	**marron (grillé)**	(roasted) chestnut
le	**pamplemousse**	grapefruit
le	**raisin**	grape(s)
le	**raisin sec**	raisin

IMPORTANT WORDS (*masculine*)

un	**arbre fruitier**	fruit tree
le	**melon**	melon

USEFUL WORDS (*masculine*)

un	**avocat**	avocado
le	**cassis**	blackcurrant
le	**kiwi**	kiwi-fruit
le	**noyau** (*pl* -x)	stone (*in fruit*)
le	**pépin**	pip (*in fruit*)
le	**pruneau** (*pl* -x)	prune

ESSENTIAL WORDS (feminine)

la	**banane**	banana
la	**cerise**	cherry
la	**fraise**	strawberry
la	**framboise**	raspberry
une	**orange**	orange
la	**peau**	skin
la	**pêche**	peach
la	**poire**	pear
la	**pomme**	apple
la	**tomate**	tomato

USEFUL WORDS (feminine)

la	**baie**	berry
la	**cacahuète**	peanut
la	**clémentine**	clementine
la	**datte**	date
la	**figue**	fig
la	**grenade**	pomegranate
la	**groseille**	redcurrant
la	**mandarine**	tangerine
la	**mûre**	blackberry
la	**myrtille**	blueberry
la	**noisette**	hazelnut
la	**noix**	nut; walnut
la	**noix de cajou**	cashew nut
la	**noix de coco**	coconut
la	**prune**	plum
la	**rhubarbe**	rhubarb
la	**vigne**	vine

USEFUL PHRASES

un jus d'orange/d'ananas an orange/a pineapple juice
une grappe de raisin a bunch of grapes
mûr(e) ripe
pas mûr(e) unripe
peler un fruit to peel a fruit
une peau de banane a banana skin

ESSENTIAL WORDS (*masculine*)

un	**abat-jour**	lampshade
le	**congélateur**	freezer
le	**fauteuil**	armchair
le	**freezer**	freezer compartment
le	**frigidaire**, le **frigo**	fridge
le	**lit**	bed
le	**meuble**	piece of furniture
les	**meubles**	furniture
le	**miroir**	mirror
le	**placard**	cupboard
le	**radiateur**	heater
le	**radio-réveil**	radio alarm
le	**réfrigérateur**	fridge
le	**téléphone**	telephone

IMPORTANT WORDS (*masculine*)

un	**appareil (ménager)**	kitchen appliance
un	**aspirateur**	vacuum cleaner
le	**buffet**	sideboard
le	**bureau** (*pl* -x)	desk
le	**canapé**	sofa
le	**canapé-lit**	sofa bed
le	**coffre**	chest
le	**four à micro-ondes**	microwave oven
le	**lave-linge**	washing machine
le	**lave-vaisselle**	dishwasher
le	**lecteur de CD/DVD**	CD/DVD player
le	**lecteur MP3**	MP3 player
le	**livre électronique**	e-book
le	**piano**	piano
le	**portable**	mobile phone
le	**sèche-linge**	tumble-dryer
le	**tableau** (*pl* -x)	picture
le	**téléphone sans fil**	cordless phone

ESSENTIAL WORDS (feminine)

une	armoire	wardrobe
la	bouilloire	kettle
la	chaîne (stéréo)	stereo system
la	chaise	chair
la	cuisinière (électrique/à gaz)	(electric/gas) cooker
la	glace	mirror
la	lampe	lamp
la	ligne fixe	landline
la	machine à laver	washing machine
la	pendule	clock
la	pièce	room
la	radio	radio
la	table	table
la	télévision	television

IMPORTANT WORDS (feminine)

la	bibliothèque	bookcase
la	liseuse	e-reader
la	peinture	painting
la	radio numérique (DAB)	digital radio
la	table basse	coffee table
la	tablette tactile	tablet

USEFUL WORDS (*masculine*)

le	**berceau** (*pl* -x)	cradle
le	**cadre**	frame
le	**caméscope**	camcorder
le	**camion de déménagement**	removal van
le	**casque**	headphones
le	**chargeur**	charger
le	**déménagement**	move
le	**déménageur**	removal man
les	**écouteurs**	earphones
le	**fer à repasser**	iron
le	**four**	oven
le	**GPS**	sat nav
le	**:home cinéma**	home cinema system
le	**lampadaire**	standard lamp
le	**lisseur (à cheveux)**	hair straighteners
le	**lit d'enfant**	cot
les	**lits superposés**	bunk beds
le	**matelas**	mattress
le	**mobilier**	furniture
le	**pèse-personne**	scales
le	**portemanteau** (*pl* -x)	coat hanger; coat rack; hat stand
le	**robot ménager**	food processor
le	**répondeur**	answering machine
le	**sèche-cheveux** (*pl inv*)	hair-dryer
le	**secrétaire**	writing desk
le	**siège**	seat
le	**store**	blind
le	**tabouret**	stool
le	**tapis**	rug
le	**tiroir**	drawer
le	**volets**	shutters
les	**vidéoprojecteur**	video projector

USEFUL PHRASES

un appartement meublé a furnished flat
allumer/éteindre le radiateur to switch on/off the heater
j'ai fait mon lit I've made my bed
s'asseoir to sit down
mettre qch au four to put sth in the oven

USEFUL WORDS *(feminine)*

une	**antenne**	aerial
une	**antenne parabolique**	satellite dish
la	**caméra vidéo**	video camera, camcorder
la	**chaîne compacte**	music centre
la	**clé USB**	USB stick
la	**coiffeuse**	dressing table
la	**commode**	chest of drawers
une	**enceinte**	speaker
une	**étagère**	shelves
la	**:hotte aspirante**	cooker hood
la	**lampe halogène**	halogen lamp
la	**machine à coudre**	sewing machine
la	**moquette**	fitted carpet
la	**planche à repasser**	ironing board
la	**table de chevet**	bedside table
la	**télécommande**	remote control

USEFUL PHRASES

tirer les rideaux to draw the curtains
fermer les volets to close the shutters
c'est un 4 pièces it's a 4-roomed flat

ESSENTIAL WORDS

les Alpes (fpl)	the Alps
l'Atlantique (m)	the Atlantic
Bordeaux	Bordeaux
la Bourgogne	Burgundy
la Bretagne	Brittany
Bruxelles	Brussels
la Côte d'Azur	the Cote d'Azur
Douvres	Dover
Édimbourg	Edinburgh
l'est (m)	the east
la Loire	the Loire
Londres	London
Lyon	Lyons
la Manche	the Channel
Marseille	Marseilles
le Massif Central	the Massif Central
la Méditerranée	the Mediterranean
la mer du Nord	the North Sea
le Midi	the South of France
le nord	the north
la Normandie	Normandy
l'ouest (m)	the west
Paris	Paris
les Pyrénées (fpl)	the Pyrenees
le Rhône	the Rhone
la Seine	the Seine
le sud	the south

IMPORTANT WORDS

Québec	Quebec (city)
le Québec	Quebec (state)
le Rhin	the Rhine
la Tamise	the Thames

USEFUL WORDS

Alger	Algiers
Anvers	Antwerp
Athènes	Athens
Barcelone	Barcelona
Berlin	Berlin
Le Caire	Cairo
la capitale	the capital
le chef-lieu	the main town
la Corse	Corsica
l'Extrême-Orient (m)	the Far East
Genève	Geneva
les îles (fpl) anglo-normandes	the Channel Islands
les îles (fpl) Britanniques	the British Isles
le Jura	the Jura Mountains
le lac Léman	Lake Geneva
Moscou	Moscow
le Moyen-Orient	the Middle East
le Pacifique	the Pacific
Pékin	Beijing
le Pôle nord/sud	the North/South Pole
le Proche-Orient	the Near East
la Sardaigne	Sardinia
Varsovie	Warsaw
Venise	Venice
Vienne	Vienna
les Vosges (fpl)	the Vosges Mountains

USEFUL PHRASES

aller à Londres/en Bourgogne to go to London/to Burgundy

aller dans le Midi to go to the South of France

je viens de Londres/du Massif Central I come from London/from the Massif Central

au nord in or to the north; **au sud** in or to the south

à l'est in or to the east; **à l'ouest** in or to the west

GREETINGS

bonjour hello
salut hi; goodbye
ça va? how are you?
ça va *(in reply)* fine
enchanté(e) pleased to meet you
allô hello *(on telephone)*
bonsoir good evening; good night
bonne nuit good night *(when going to bed)*
au revoir goodbye
à demain see you tomorrow
à bientôt see you soon
à tout à l'heure see you later
adieu farewell

BEST WISHES

bon anniversaire happy birthday
joyeux Noël merry Christmas
bonne année happy New Year
joyeuses Pâques happy Easter
meilleurs vœux best wishes
bienvenue welcome
félicitations congratulations
bon appétit enjoy your meal
bon courage all the best
bonne chance good luck
bon voyage safe journey
à tes *(or* **vos***)* **souhaits** bless you *(after a sneeze)*
à la tienne *(or* **la vôtre***)* cheers
à ta *(or* **votre***)* **santé** cheers

SURPRISE

mon Dieu my goodness
comment?, hein?, quoi? what?
ah bon oh, I see
ça, par exemple well, well
sans blague(?) really(?)
ah oui?, c'est vrai?, vraiment? really?
tu rigoles, tu plaisantes you're kidding
quelle chance! what a stroke of luck!
tiens! well, well!

POLITENESS

excusez-moi I'm sorry, excuse me
s'il vous (*or* **te) plaît** please
SVP please
merci thank you
non merci no thank you; **oui merci** yes please
de rien, je vous en prie, il n'y a pas de quoi not at all, it's quite all right,
  don't mention it
volontiers gladly

AGREEMENT

oui yes
bien sûr of course
d'accord OK
bon fine

DISAGREEMENT

non no
mais non no (*contradicting a positive statement*)
si yes (*contradicting a negative statement*)
bien sûr que non of course not
jamais de la vie not on your life
pas du tout not at all
au contraire on the contrary
ça, par exemple well I never
quel culot what a cheek
mêlez-vous de vos affaires mind your own business

DIFFICULTIES

au secours help
au feu fire
aïe ouch
pardon (I'm) sorry, excuse me, I beg your pardon
je m'excuse I'm sorry
je regrette I'm sorry
désolé(e) I'm (really) sorry
c'est dommage, quel dommage what a pity
zut bother
j'en ai marre I'm fed up
je n'en peux plus I can't stand it any more
oh là là oh dear
quelle horreur how awful

ORDERS

attention! be careful!
hep *or* **eh, vous là-bas!** hey, you there!
fiche le camp! clear off!
chut! shhhh!
ça suffit! that's enough!
défense de fumer no smoking
allez go on, come on
allons-y let's go
allez-y, vas-y go ahead

OTHERS

aucune idée no idea
peut-être perhaps, maybe
je ne sais pas I don't know
vous désirez? can I help you?
voilà there, there you are
j'arrive just coming
ne t'en fais pas don't worry
ce n'est pas la peine it's not worth it
à propos by the way
dis donc (*or* **dites donc**) by the way
chéri(e) darling
le (*or* **la**) **pauvre** poor thing
tant mieux so much the better
ça m'est égal I don't mind
tant pis too bad
ça dépend that depends
que faire? what shall I (or we) do?
à quoi bon? what's the point?
ça m'embête it bothers me
ça m'agace it gets on my nerves

ESSENTIAL WORDS (*masculine*)

un	**accident**	accident
le	**dentiste** (*m+f*)	dentist
le	**docteur** (*m+f*)	doctor
un	**hôpital** (*pl* hôpitaux)	hospital
un	**infirmier**	(male) nurse
le	**lit**	bed
le	**malade**	patient
le	**médecin** (*m+f*)	doctor
le	**rendez-vous** (*pl inv*)	appointment
le	**ventre**	stomach

IMPORTANT WORDS (*masculine*)

un	**antiseptique**	antiseptic
le	**brancard**	stretcher
le	**cabinet (de consultation)**	surgery
le	**cachet**	tablet
le	**comprimé**	tablet
le	**coton hydrophile**	cotton wool
le	**coup de soleil**	sunburn
le	**médicament**	medicine, drug
le	**pansement**	dressing; bandage
le	**patient**	patient
le	**pharmacien**	chemist
le	**plâtre**	plaster (cast)
le	**remède**	medicine
un	**rhume**	cold
le	**sang**	blood
le	**sirop**	syrup
le	**sparadrap**	sticking plaster

USEFUL PHRASES

il y a eu un accident there's been an accident
être admis(e) à l'hôpital to be admitted to hospital
vous devez rester au lit you must stay in bed
être malade, être souffrant(e) to be ill
je suis diabétique I am diabetic
se sentir mieux to feel better
soigner to look after

ESSENTIAL WORDS (*feminine*)

une	**aspirine**	aspirin
une	**infirmière**	nurse
la	**pastille**	lozenge
la	**pharmacie**	chemist's
la	**santé**	health
la	**température**	temperature

IMPORTANT WORDS (*feminine*)

une	**allergie**	allergy
une	**ambulance**	ambulance
une	**assurance**	insurance
la	**blessure**	injury, wound
la	**chambre d'hôpital**	hospital room
la	**clinique**	clinic, private hospital
la	**crème**	cream, ointment
la	**cuillerée**	spoonful
la	**diarrhée**	diarrhoea
la	**douleur**	pain
la	**grippe**	flu
la	**grippe porcine**	swine flu
une	**insolation**	sunstroke
la	**maladie**	illness
une	**opération**	operation
une	**ordonnance**	prescription
la	**patiente**	patient
la	**pilule**	pill; the Pill
la	**piqûre**	injection; sting
la	**réaction allergique**	allergic reaction
les	**urgences**	Accident and Emergency

USEFUL PHRASES

je me suis blessé(e), je me suis fait mal I have hurt myself
je me suis coupé le doigt I have cut my finger
je me suis foulé la cheville I have sprained my ankle
il s'est cassé le bras he has broken his arm
je me suis brûlé I have burnt myself
j'ai mal à la gorge/mal à la tête/mal au ventre I've got a sore throat/
a headache/a stomach ache
avoir de la température *or* **de la fièvre** to have a temperature

USEFUL WORDS (*masculine*)

un	**abcès**	abscess
un	**accès**	fit
le	**bandage**	bandage
le	**bleu**	bruise
le	**cancer**	cancer
le	**choc**	shock
le	**dentier**	false teeth
le	**fauteuil roulant**	wheelchair
le	**fortifiant**	tonic
le	**microbe**	germ
le	**nerf**	nerve
les	**oreillons**	mumps
le	**poison**	poison
le	**pouls** [pu]	pulse
les	**premiers secours**	first aid
les	**premiers soins**	first aid
le	**préservatif**	condom
le	**régime**	diet
le	**repos**	rest
le	**rhume des foins**	hayfever
le	**SAMU**	emergency medical service
le	**sida**	AIDS
le	**stress**	stress
le	**vertige**	dizzy spell

USEFUL PHRASES

j'ai mal au cœur I feel sick
maigrir to lose weight
grossir to put on weight
avaler to swallow
saigner to bleed
vomir to vomit
être en forme to be in good shape
se reposer to rest

USEFUL WORDS (*feminine*)

	l'**acné**	acne
une	**angine**	tonsillitis
une	**appendicite**	appendicitis
la	**béquille**	crutch
la	**carte européenne** **d'assurance maladie**	European health insurance card
la	**cicatrice**	scar
la	**coqueluche**	whooping cough
la	**crise cardiaque**	heart attack
une	**écharde**	splinter
une	**égratignure**	scratch
une	**épidémie**	epidemic
la	**grossesse**	pregnancy
la	**guérison**	recovery
la	**migraine**	migraine
la	**nausée**	nausea
la	**pandémie**	pandemic
la	**plaie**	wound
la	**pommade**	ointment
la	**radio**	X-ray
la	**rougeole**	measles
la	**rubéole**	German measles
la	**toux**	cough
la	**transfusion**	blood transfusion
la	**varicelle**	chickenpox
la	**variole**	smallpox

USEFUL PHRASES

guérir to cure; to get better
grièvement blessé(e) seriously injured
êtes-vous assuré(e)? are you insured?
je suis enrhumé(e) I have a cold
ça fait mal! that hurts!
respirer to breathe; **s'évanouir** to faint
tousser to cough; **mourir** to die
perdre connaissance to lose consciousness
avoir le bras en écharpe to have one's arm in a sling

ESSENTIAL WORDS (masculine)

un	ascenseur	lift
les	bagages	luggage
le	balcon	balcony
le	bar	bar
le	bruit	noise
le	chèque	cheque
le	client	guest
le	confort	comfort
le	déjeuner	lunch
le	directeur	manager
un	escalier	stairs
un	étage	floor; storey
le	garçon	waiter
le	grand lit	double bed
un	hôtel	hotel
les	lits jumeaux	twin beds
le	numéro	number
le	passeport	passport
le	petit déjeuner	breakfast
le	porteur	porter
le	prix	price
le	réceptionniste	receptionist
le	repas	meal
le	restaurant	restaurant
le	rez-de-chaussée	ground floor
le	séjour	stay
le	tarif	rates
le	téléphone	telephone
les	WC	toilets
le	wifi	wifi

USEFUL PHRASES

je voudrais réserver une chambre I would like to book a room
une chambre avec douche/avec salle de bains a room with a shower/
   with a bathroom
une chambre pour une personne a single room
une chambre pour deux personnes a double room

ESSENTIAL WORDS *(feminine)*

	l'**addition**	bill
les	**arrhes** [AR]	deposit
la	**carte bancaire**	bank card
la	**chambre**	room
la	**clé, clef**	key
la	**cliente**	guest
la	**date**	date
la	**directrice**	manageress
la	**douche**	shower
	l'**entrée**	entrance
la	**fiche**	form
la	**monnaie**	change
la	**note**	bill
la	**nuit**	night
la	**pension**	guesthouse
la	**pension complète**	full board
la	**piscine**	swimming pool
la	**réception**	reception
la	**réceptionniste**	receptionist
la	**réservation**	reservation, booking
la	**salle de bains**	bathroom
la	**serviette (de toilette)**	towel
la	**serveuse**	waitress
la	**sortie de secours**	fire escape
la	**télévision**	television
les	**toilettes**	toilets
la	**valise**	suitcase
la	**vue**	view

USEFUL PHRASES

nous avons réservé en ligne we made a booking online
avez-vous une pièce d'identité? do you have any ID?
à quelle heure est le petit déjeuner? what time is breakfast served?
faire la chambre to clean the room
"ne pas déranger" "do not disturb"

IMPORTANT WORDS (*masculine*)

un	**accueil**	welcome
le	**bouton**	switch
le	**cabinet de toilette**	toilet
le	**coffre-fort**	safe
le	**digicode**	entry code
les	**draps**	sheets
le	**guide**	guidebook
le	**pourboire**	tip
le	**prix net**	inclusive price
le	**reçu**	receipt

USEFUL WORDS (*masculine*)

le	**cuisinier**	cook
le	**forfait**	package (deal)
le	**:hall**	foyer
un	**hôtelier**	hotelier
le	**maître d'hôtel**	head waiter
le	**parking**	car park
le	**pensionnaire**	guest (at guesthouse)
le	**sommelier**	wine waiter

USEFUL PHRASES

occupé(e) occupied
libre vacant
propre clean
sale dirty
dormir to sleep
se réveiller to wake
"tout confort" "with all facilities"
pourriez-vous me réveiller à 7 heures demain matin? I'd like a 7 o'clock alarm call tomorrow morning, please
une chambre donnant sur la mer a room overlooking the sea

IMPORTANT WORDS *(feminine)*

une **auberge**	inn
la **carte magnétique**	electronic key card
la **demi-pension** *(pl ~s)*	half-board
la **femme de chambre**	chambermaid
la **réclamation**	complaint
la **pension de famille**	guesthouse
la **pensionnaire**	guest (at guesthouse)

USEFUL PHRASES

chambre avec demi-pension room with breakfast and dinner provided
on se met à la terrasse? shall we sit outside?
on nous a servis à la terrasse we were served outside
un hôtel 3 étoiles a three-star hotel
TTC (toutes taxes comprises) inclusive of tax

ESSENTIAL WORDS (*masculine*)

un	appartement	flat
un	ascenseur	lift
le	balcon	balcony
le	bâtiment	building
le	chauffage central	central heating
le	confort	comfort
un	escalier	stairs
un	étage	floor; storey
	l'extérieur	exterior
le	garage	garage
un	grand ensemble	housing estate
un	HLM (habitation à loyer modéré)	council flat *or* house
un	immeuble	block of flats
	l'intérieur	interior
le	jardin	garden
le	meuble	piece of furniture
les	meubles	furniture
le	mur	wall
le	numéro de téléphone	phone number
le	parking	car park
le	rez-de-chaussée (*pl inv*)	ground floor
le	salon	living room
le	séjour	living room
le	sous-sol (*pl ~s*)	basement
le	terrain	plot of land
le	village	village

USEFUL PHRASES
quand je rentre à la maison when I go home
regarder par la fenêtre to look out of the window
chez moi/toi/nous at my/your/our house
déménager to move house
louer un appartement to rent a flat

ESSENTIAL WORDS (*feminine*)

une	**adresse**	address
une	**allée**	avenue, drive
une	**avenue**	avenue
la	**cave**	cellar
la	**chambre (à coucher)**	bedroom
la	**clé, clef**	key
la	**cuisine**	kitchen
la	**douche**	shower
	l'**entrée**	entrance
la	**fenêtre**	window
une	**HLM (habitation à loyer modéré)**	council flat *or* house
la	**maison**	house
la	**pièce**	room
la	**porte**	door
la	**porte d'entrée**	front door
la	**rue**	street
la	**salle à manger**	dining room
la	**salle de bains**	bathroom
la	**salle de séjour**	living room
la	**salle**	room
les	**toilettes**	toilet
la	**ville**	town
la	**vue**	view

USEFUL PHRASES
j'habite un appartement/une maison I live in a flat/a house
en haut upstairs
en bas downstairs
au premier on the first floor
au rez-de-chaussée on the ground floor
à la maison at home

IMPORTANT WORDS (*masculine*)

l'ameublement	furniture
le **cabinet de toilette**	toilet
le **concierge**	caretaker
le **couloir**	corridor
le **débarras**	storage cupboard
le **déménagement**	move
l'entretien	upkeep
le **gîte**	holiday home
le **logement**	accommodation
le **loyer**	rent
le **meublé**	furnished flat
le **palier**	landing
le **propriétaire**	owner; landlord
le **toit**	roof
le **voisin**	neighbour

USEFUL WORDS (*masculine*)

le **bureau**	study
le **carreau** (*pl* -x)	tile; windowpane
le **décor**	decoration
le **grenier**	attic
le **locataire**	tenant; lodger
le **parquet**	parquet floor
le **pavillon**	house
le **plafond**	ceiling
le **plancher**	floor
le **seuil**	doorstep
le **store**	blind
le **studio**	studio flat
le **tuyau** (*pl* -x)	pipe
le **vestibule**	hall
le **volet**	shutter

USEFUL PHRASES

frapper à la porte to knock at the door
on a sonné the doorbell's just gone

IMPORTANT WORDS *(feminine)*

la	**cheminée**	chimney; fireplace
la	**concierge**	caretaker
la	**cour**	yard
la	**femme de ménage**	cleaner
la	**fumée**	smoke
la	**pelouse**	lawn
la	**propriétaire**	owner; landlady
la	**voisine**	neighbour

USEFUL WORDS *(feminine)*

une	**antenne**	aerial
une	**ardoise**	slate
la	**chambre d'amis**	spare room
la	**chaudière**	boiler
la	**façade**	front (*of house*)
la	**:haie**	hedge
la	**locataire**	tenant; lodger
la	**loge**	caretaker's room
la	**lucarne**	skylight
la	**mansarde**	attic
la	**marche**	step
la	**paroi**	partition
la	**porte-fenêtre** (*pl* ~s~s)	French window
la	**sonnette**	door bell
la	**tuile**	roof tile
la	**vitre**	window pane

USEFUL PHRASES
de l'extérieur from the outside
à l'intérieur on the inside
jusqu'au plafond up to the ceiling

ESSENTIAL WORDS *(masculine)*

le	**bouton**	switch
le	**cendrier**	ashtray
le	**dentifrice**	toothpaste
le	**drap**	sheet
un	**essuie-mains** *(pl inv)*	hand towel
un	**évier**	sink
le	**gaz**	gas
le	**lavabo**	washbasin
le	**lecteur de DVD**	DVD player
le	**ménage**	housework
le	**miroir**	mirror
un	**oreiller**	pillow
le	**placard**	cupboard
le	**plateau** *(pl -x)*	tray
le	**poster** [pɔstɛʀ]	poster
le	**radiateur**	heater
le	**réveil**	alarm clock
les	**rideaux**	curtains
le	**robinet**	tap
le	**savon**	soap
le	**tableau**	picture
le	**tapis**	rug
le	**téléviseur**	television set

USEFUL PHRASES

prendre un bain, se baigner to have a bath
prendre une douche to have a shower
faire le ménage to do the housework
j'aime faire la cuisine I like cooking

ESSENTIAL WORDS *(feminine)*

une **armoire**	wardrobe
la **baignoire**	bath
la **balance**	scales
la **boîte aux lettres**	letterbox
la **brosse**	brush
la **cafetière**	coffee pot; coffee maker
la **casserole**	saucepan
la **chaîne hi-fi**	hi-fi
la **couverture**	blanket
la **cuisinière**	cooker
la **douche**	shower
l'**eau**	water
l'**électricité**	electricity
la **glace**	mirror
la **lampe**	lamp
la **lumière**	light
la **machine à laver**	washing machine
la **photo**	photo
la **poubelle**	dustbin
la **radio**	radio
la **serviette**	towel; napkin
la **télévision**	TV, television
la **vaisselle**	dishes

USEFUL PHRASES

regarder la télévision to watch television
à la télévision on television
allumer/éteindre la télévision to switch on/off the TV
jeter qch à la poubelle to throw sth in the dustbin
faire la vaisselle to do the dishes

IMPORTANT WORDS (*masculine*)

un	**aspirateur**	vacuum cleaner
le	**bidet**	bidet
le	**four**	oven
le	**lave-vaisselle** (*pl inv*)	dishwasher
le	**linge**	bedclothes; washing

USEFUL WORDS (*masculine*)

le	**balai**	broom
le	**bibelot**	ornament
le	**chiffon**	duster
le	**cintre**	coat hanger
le	**coussin**	cushion
le	**couvercle**	lid
le	**fer à repasser**	iron
le	**four à micro-ondes**	microwave oven
le	**grille-pain** (*pl inv*)	toaster
un	**interrupteur**	switch
le	**mixeur**	blender
le	**moulin à café**	coffee grinder
le	**papier peint**	wallpaper
le	**seau** (*pl* -x)	bucket
le	**torchon**	dishcloth
le	**traversin**	bolster
le	**vase**	vase

USEFUL PHRASES

brancher/débrancher to plug in/to unplug
passer l'aspirateur to hoover
faire la lessive to do the washing

IMPORTANT WORDS (feminine)

une	ampoule électrique	light bulb
la	baignoire	bath
la	femme de ménage	cleaner
la	lessive	washing powder; washing
la	peinture	paint; painting
la	poêle [pwal]	frying pan
la	poussière	dust
la	prise de courant	socket
la	recette	recipe
la	serrure	lock

USEFUL WORDS (feminine)

la	bouilloire	kettle
la	cocotte-minute® (pl ~s~)	pressure cooker
la	corbeille à papier	waste paper basket
la	couette	duvet
la	couverture chauffante	electric blanket
la	descente de lit	bedside rug
une	échelle	ladder
une	éponge	sponge
la	moquette	fitted carpet
les	ordures	rubbish
la	planche à repasser	ironing board
la	poignée	handle
la	tapisserie	wallpaper

USEFUL PHRASES

balayer to sweep (up)
nettoyer to clean
ranger ses affaires to tidy away one's things
laisser traîner ses affaires to leave one's things lying about

ESSENTIAL WORDS *(masculine)*

un	abonnement (téléphonique)	phone contract
un	appel	call
le	billet	ticket; banknote
le	bureau (pl -x) de change	bureau de change
le	centime (d'euro)	euro cent
le	chèque	cheque
le	code postal	postcode
le	colis	parcel
le	courriel	email
le	cybercafé	internet café
le	DAB (distributeur automatique de billets)	cashpoint, ATM
un	employé	counter clerk
un	euro	euro
le	facteur	postman
le	franc suisse	Swiss franc
le	guichet	counter
un	indicatif	dialling code
le	justificatif	written proof
un	mail	email
le	numéro	number
un	office du tourisme	tourist information office
un	opérateur	phone company
le	paquet	parcel
le	passeport	passport
le	prix	price
les	renseignements	information; directory enquiries
le	répondeur	answerphone
le	SMS	text message
le	stylo	pen
le	syndicat d'initiative	tourist information office
le	tarif	(postage) rate
le	téléphone	telephone
le	(téléphone) fixe	landline
le	(téléphone) portable	mobile (phone)
le	timbre	stamp

USEFUL PHRASES

la banque la plus proche the nearest bank
je voudrais encaisser un chèque/changer de l'argent I would like to cash a cheque/change some money

ESSENTIAL WORDS *(feminine)*

une	**adresse**	address
les	**arrhes**	deposit
la	**banque**	bank
la	**boîte aux lettres**	postbox
la	**boîte vocale**	voicemail
la	**caisse**	check-out
la	**carte d'identité**	ID card
la	**carte postale**	postcard
une	**enveloppe**	envelope
une	**erreur**	mistake
la	**factrice**	postwoman
la	**fiche**	form
la	**lettre**	letter
la	**livre sterling**	pound sterling
la	**monnaie**	change
la	**pièce d'identité**	ID
la	**poste**	post office
la	**réponse**	reply
la	**signature**	signature
la	**sonnerie**	ringtone
la	**tonalité**	dialling tone

USEFUL PHRASES

un coup de téléphone *or* **de fil** a phone call
téléphoner à qn to phone sb
décrocher to lift the receiver
composer le numéro to dial (the number)
allô – ici Jean *or* **c'est Jean à l'appareil** hello – this is Jean
la ligne est occupée the line is engaged
ne quittez pas hold the line
je me suis trompé(e) de numéro I got the wrong number
raccrocher to hang up
je voudrais appeler à l'étranger I'd like to make an international
  phone call

IMPORTANT WORDS (*masculine*)

un	**annuaire**	telephone directory
le	**carnet de chèques**	cheque book
le	**chèque de voyage**	traveller's cheque
le	**compte (en banque)**	(bank) account
le	**coup de téléphone**	phone call
le	**courrier**	mail
le	**crédit**	credit
le	**domicile**	home address
le	**formulaire**	form
le	**:haut débit**	broadband
le	**mail**	email
les	**objets trouvés**	lost property office
le	**paiement**	payment
le	**papier à lettres**	writing paper
le	**portefeuille**	wallet
le	**porte-monnaie** (*pl inv*)	purse
le	**supplément**	extra charge
le	**taux de change**	exchange rate
le	**télégramme**	telegram
le	**wifi**	wifi

USEFUL WORDS (*masculine*)

un	**accusé de réception**	acknowledgement of receipt
le	**combiné**	receiver
le	**destinataire**	addressee
l'	**expéditeur**	sender
un	**identifiant**	login
un	**imprimé**	printed matter
le	**mandat**	postal order
le	**mot de passe**	password
le	**numéro vert**	Freefone® number
le	**papier d'emballage**	wrapping paper
le	**récepteur**	receiver
le	**standardiste**	operator
le	**tampon**	stamp

IMPORTANT WORDS *(feminine)*

une	**adresse électronique**	email address
la	**cabine téléphonique**	callbox
la	**carte bancaire**	bank card
la	**Carte bleue®**	debit card
la	**carte SIM**	SIM card
la	**carte téléphonique**	phone card; top up card
la	**dépense**	expense
la	**fente**	slot
la	**levée**	collection
une	**opératrice**	operator
la	**pièce jointe**	attachment
la	**poste restante**	poste restante
la	**récompense**	reward
la	**taxe**	tax

USEFUL WORDS *(feminine)*

la	**boîte postale**	PO box
la	**communication interurbaine**	inter-city call
la	**communication locale**	local call
l'	**horloge parlante**	speaking clock
la	**lettre recommandée**	registered letter
la	**standardiste**	switchboard operator
la	**télécarte®**	phonecard

USEFUL PHRASES

j'ai perdu mon portefeuille I've lost my wallet
remplir une fiche to fill in a form
en majuscules in block letters
téléphoner en PCV to make a reverse charge call

GENERAL SITUATIONS

quelle est votre adresse? what is your address?
comment ça s'écrit? how do you spell that?
avez-vous la monnaie de 10 euros? do you have change of 10 euros?
écrire to write
répondre to reply
signer to sign
est-ce que vous pouvez m'aider? can you help me please?
pour aller à la gare? how do I get to the station?
tout droit straight on
à droite to or on the right; **à gauche** to or on the left

LETTERS

Cher Robert Dear Robert
Chère Anne Dear Anne
Monsieur Dear Sir
Madame (or **Mademoiselle**) Dear Madam
amitiés best wishes
bien affectueusement love from
bien amicalement or **cordialement** kind regards
grosses bises love and kisses
veuillez agréer mes (or **nos**) **salutations distinguées** yours faithfully
je vous prie d'agréer, Monsieur (or **Madame**), **l'expression de mes
sentiments les meilleurs** yours sincerely
TSVP PTO

MOBILES

envoyer un SMS à qn to text sb
envoyer un MMS photo à qn to send a picture message
envoyer un MMS vidéo à qn to send a video message
télécharger une sonnerie to download a ringtone
Je ne te capte plus! You're breaking up!
Je n'ai plus de crédit. I'm out of credit.
Je n'ai pas de réseau. I can't get a network.

EMAIL

composer un mail to compose an email
envoyer un mail à qn to send an email to sb
faire suivre un mail to forward an email
joindre un fichier à un mail to attach a file to an email
répondre à un mail to reply to an email

ESSENTIAL WORDS *(masculine)*

un	**accident**	accident
un	**agent (de police)**	policeman
le	**cambriolage**	burglary
le	**commissariat de police**	police station
un	**incendie**	fire
le	**problème**	problem

IMPORTANT WORDS *(masculine)*

un	**agresseur**	attacker
un	**avocat**	lawyer
le	**cambrioleur**	burglar
le	**constat**	report
le	**consulat**	consulate
le	**coupable**	culprit
les	**dégâts**	damage
le(s)	**dommage(s)**	damage
un	**espion**	spy
le	**gendarme**	policeman
le	**gouvernement**	government
les	**impôts**	income tax
le	**mort**	dead man
le	**piratage**	hacking
le	**porte-monnaie** *(pl inv)*	purse
le	**portefeuille**	wallet
le	**poste de police**	police station
le	**propriétaire**	owner
le	**témoin**	witness
le	**viol**	rape
le	**vol**	robbery
le	**voleur**	thief

USEFUL PHRASES

voler to steal; to rob
cambrioler to burgle
on m'a volé mon portefeuille! someone has stolen my wallet!
contraire à la loi illegal
ce n'est pas de ma faute it's not my fault
au secours! help!

ESSENTIAL WORDS (*feminine*)

la	**faute**	fault
	l'**identité**	identity
la	**pièce d'identité**	ID
la	**vérité**	truth
la	**victime**	victim

IMPORTANT WORDS (*feminine*)

une	**agression**	assault
une	**ambassade**	embassy
une	**amende**	fine
une	**armée**	army
une	**avocate**	lawyer
la	**bande**	gang
la	**coupable**	culprit
la	**fraude**	fraud
la	**fraude fiscale**	tax evasion
la	**gendarmerie**	police station
les	**incivilités**	antisocial behaviour
la	**manifestation**	demonstration
la	**mort**	death
la	**morte**	dead woman
la	**permission**	permission
la	**police d'assurance**	insurance policy
la	**propriétaire**	owner
la	**récompense**	reward
	l'**usurpation d'identité**	identity theft
la	**violence**	violence

USEFUL PHRASES

au voleur! stop thief!
au feu! fire!
braquer une banque to rob a bank
police-secours emergency services
incarcérer to imprison
innocent(e) innocent
s'évader to escape

USEFUL WORDS (*masculine*)

un	**assassin**	murderer
le	**butin**	loot
le	**cadavre**	corpse
le	**coup (de feu)**	(gun) shot
le	**courage**	bravery
le	**crime**	crime
le	**criminel**	criminal
le	**dealer**	drug dealer
le	**détective privé**	private detective
le	**détournement d'avion**	plane hijacking
le	**drogué**	drug addict
un	**enlèvement**	kidnapping
un	**escroc** [ɛskʀo]	crook
le	**flic**	cop
le	**fusil** [fyzi]	gun
le	**gangster**	gangster
le	**garde**	guard
le	**gardien**	guard; warden
le	**:héros**	hero
le	**:hold-up** (*pl inv*)	hold-up
le	**juge**	judge
le	**jury**	jury
le	**meurtre**	murder
le	**meurtrier**	murderer
un	**otage**	hostage
le	**palais de justice**	law courts
le	**pirate de l'air**	hijacker
le	**policier**	policeman
le	**prisonnier**	prisoner
le	**procès**	trial
le	**PV**	fine
le	**reportage**	report
le	**revolver** [ʀevɔlvɛʀ]	revolver
le	**sauvetage**	rescue
le	**témoignage**	evidence
le	**témoin**	witness
le	**terrorisme**	terrorism
le	**terroriste**	terrorist
le	**tribunal**	court
le	**voyou**	hooligan

USEFUL WORDS *(feminine)*

	l'**accusation**	the prosecution
une	**accusation**	charge; accusation
une	**arme**	weapon
une	**arrestation**	arrest
la	**bagarre**	fight
la	**bombe**	bomb
la	**cellule**	cell
la	**défense**	defence
la	**déposition**	statement
la	**dispute**	argument
la	**droguée**	drug addict
les	**drogues**	drugs
une	**émeute**	uprising
une	**enquête**	inquiry
une	**évasion**	escape
	l'**héroïne**	heroine; heroin
	l'**incarcération**	imprisonment
la	**loi**	law
une	**ordonnance**	police order
la	**preuve**	proof
la	**prison**	prison
la	**rafle**	raid
la	**rançon**	ransom
la	**tentative**	attempt

USEFUL PHRASES

une attaque à main armée a hold-up
enlever un enfant to abduct a child
se battre to fight
une bande de voyous a bunch of hooligans
en prison in prison
arrêter to arrest
inculper to charge
être en détention provisoire to be remanded in custody
mettre qn en examen to indict sb
prendre la fuite to run away

ESSENTIAL WORDS (masculine)

l'acier	steel
l'argent	silver
le bois	wood
le coton	cotton
le cuir	leather
le fer	iron
le gas-oil	diesel
le gaz	gas
le métal (pl métaux)	metal
l'or	gold
le plastique	plastic
le tissu	fabric
le verre	glass

IMPORTANT WORDS (masculine)

l'acier inoxydable	stainless steel
l'aluminium	aluminium
le carton	cardboard
l'état	condition
le fer forgé	wrought iron
le papier	paper
le synthétique	synthetics
le tissu	fabric

USEFUL PHRASES

une chaise de *or* en bois a wooden chair
une boîte en plastique a plastic box
une bague d'or *or* en or a gold ring
en bon état in good condition
en mauvais état in bad condition

ESSENTIAL WORDS (feminine)

la	**fourrure**	fur
la	**laine**	wool
la	**pierre**	stone

IMPORTANT WORDS (feminine)

la	**brique**	brick
la	**soie**	silk

USEFUL PHRASES
un manteau en fourrure a fur coat
un pull en laine a woolly jumper
rouillé(e) rusty

USEFUL WORDS (*masculine*)

l'**acrylique**	acrylic
le **béton**	concrete
le **bronze**	bronze
le **caoutchouc** [kautʃu]	rubber
le **caoutchouc mousse**	foam rubber
le **charbon**	coal
le **ciment**	cement
le **cristal**	crystal
le **cuivre**	copper
le **cuivre jaune**	brass
le **daim**	suede
l'**étain**	tin; pewter
le **fer-blanc**	tin, tinplate
le **fil**	thread
le **fil de fer**	wire
le **lin**	linen
le **liquide**	liquid
le **marbre**	marble
les **matériaux**	materials
l'**osier**	wickerwork
le **plâtre**	plaster
le **plomb**	lead
le **satin**	satin
le **velours**	velvet
le **velours côtelé**	corduroy

USEFUL WORDS (*feminine*)

l'argile	clay
la cire	wax
la colle	glue
la dentelle	lace
une étoffe	material
la faïence	ceramics
la ficelle	string
la paille	straw
la porcelaine	china
la toile	linen; canvas

ESSENTIAL WORDS (*masculine*)

le	**CD**	CD
le	**chef d'orchestre**	conductor
le	**groupe**	group, band
un	**instrument de musique**	musical instrument
le	**musicien**	musician
un	**orchestre**	orchestra
le	**piano**	piano
le	**violon**	violin

USEFUL WORDS (*masculine*)

un	**accord**	chord
un	**accordéon**	accordion
un	**alto**	viola
un	**archet**	bow
le	**basson**	bassoon
le	**biniou**	Breton bagpipes
les	**bois**	woodwind
le	**clairon**	bugle
le	**cor**	horn
les	**cuivres**	brass
un	**enregistrement numérique**	digital recording
un	**étui**	case
un	**harmonica**	harmonica
le	**:hautbois**	oboe
le	**jazz** [dʒaz]	jazz
le	**microphone**	microphone
un	**orgue**	organ
le	**pupitre**	music stand
le	**saxophone**	saxophone
le	**solfège**	music theory
le	**soliste**	soloist
le	**studio d'enregistrement**	recording studio
le	**tambour**	drum
le	**tambourin**	tambourine
le	**triangle**	triangle
le	**trombone**	trombone
le	**violoncelle**	cello

ESSENTIAL WORDS (feminine)

la	**batterie**	drums, drum kit
la	**clarinette**	clarinet
la	**flûte**	flute
la	**flûte à bec**	recorder
la	**guitare**	guitar
la	**musique**	music

USEFUL WORDS (feminine)

la	**composition**	composition
la	**contrebasse**	double bass
la	**corde**	string
les	**cordes**	brass
la	**cornemuse**	bagpipes
les	**cymbales**	cymbals
la	**fanfare**	brass band; fanfare
la	**grosse caisse**	bass drum
la	**:harpe**	harpe
la	**note**	note
la	**soliste**	soloist
la	**sono**	PA system
la	**table de mixage**	(mixing) deck
la	**touche**	(piano) key
la	**trompette**	trumpet

USEFUL PHRASES

jouer or **interpréter un morceau** to play a piece
jouer fort/doucement to play loudly/softly
jouer juste/faux to play in tune/out of tune
jouer du piano/de la guitare to play the piano/the guitar
faire de la batterie to play drums
Luc à la batterie Luc on drums
travailler son piano to practise the piano
est-ce que tu joues dans un groupe? do you play in a band?
une fausse note a wrong note

CARDINAL NUMBERS

zéro	0	zero
un (m), une (f)	1	one
deux	2	two
trois	3	three
quatre	4	four
cinq	5	five
six	6	six
sept	7	seven
huit	8	eight
neuf	9	nine
dix	10	ten
onze	11	eleven
douze	12	twelve
treize	13	thirteen
quatorze	14	fourteen
quinze	15	fifteen
seize	16	sixteen
dix-sept	17	seventeen
dix-huit	18	eighteen
dix-neuf	19	nineteen
vingt	20	twenty
vingt et un	21	twenty-one
vingt-deux	22	twenty-two
vingt-trois	23	twenty-three
trente	30	thirty
trente et un	31	thirty-one
trente-deux	32	thirty-two
quarante	40	forty
cinquante	50	fifty
soixante	60	sixty
soixante-dix	70	seventy
soixante et onze	71	seventy-one
quatre-vingts	80	eighty
quatre-vingt-un	81	eighty-one
quatre-vingt-dix	90	ninety
quatre-vingt-onze	91	ninety-one
cent	100	one hundred

CARDINAL NUMBERS *(continued)*

cent un	**101**	a hundred and one
cent deux	**102**	a hundred and two
cent dix	**110**	a hundred and ten
cent quatre-vingt-deux	**182**	a hundred and eighty-two
deux cents	**200**	two hundred
deux cent un	**201**	two hundred and one
deux cent deux	**202**	two hundred and two
trois cents	**300**	three hundred
quatre cents	**400**	four hundred
cinq cents	**500**	five hundred
six cents	**600**	six hundred
sept cents	**700**	seven hundred
huit cents	**800**	eight hundred
neuf cents	**900**	nine hundred
mille	**1000**	one thousand
mille un	**1001**	a thousand and one
mille deux	**1002**	a thousand and two
deux mille	**2000**	two thousand
deux mille deux	**2002**	two thousand and two
dix mille	**10000**	ten thousand
cent mille	**100000**	one hundred thousand
un million	**1000000**	one million
deux millions	**2000000**	two million

USEFUL PHRASES

mille euros a thousand euros
un million de dollars one million dollars
trois virgule deux (3,2) three point two (3.2)

ORDINAL NUMBERS

premier(ière)	$1^{er}, 1^{ère}$	first
deuxième	2^e	second
troisième	3^e	third
quatrième	4^e	fourth
cinquième	5^e	fifth
sixième	6^e	sixth
septième	7^e	seventh
huitième	8^e	eighth
neuvième	9^e	ninth
dixième	10^e	tenth
onzième	11^e	eleventh
douzième	12^e	twelfth
treizième	13^e	thirteenth
quatorzième	14^e	fourteenth
quinzième	15^e	fifteenth
seizième	16^e	sixteenth
dix-septième	17^e	seventeenth
dix-huitième	18^e	eighteenth
dix-neuvième	19^e	nineteenth
vingtième	20^e	twentieth
vingt et unième	21^e	twenty-first
vingt-deuxième	22^e	twenty-second
trentième	30^e	thirtieth
trente et unième	31^e	thirty-first
quarantième	40^e	fortieth
cinquantième	50^e	fiftieth
soixantième	60^e	sixtieth
soixante-dixième	70^e	seventieth
quatre-vingtième	80^e	eightieth
quatre-vingt-dixième	90^e	ninetieth
centième	100^e	hundredth

ORDINAL NUMBERS *(continued)*

cent unième	101^e	hundred and first
cent-dixième	110^e	hundred and tenth
deux centième	200^e	two hundredth
trois centième	300^e	three hundredth
quatre centième	400^e	four hundredth
cinq centième	500^e	five hundredth
six centième	600^e	six hundredth
sept centième	700^e	seven hundredth
huit centième	800^e	eight hundredth
neuf centième	900^e	nine hundredth
millième	1000^e	thousandth
deux millième	2000^e	two thousandth
millionième	1000000^e	millionth
deux millionième	2000000^e	two millionth

FRACTIONS

un(e) demi(e)	$\frac{1}{2}$	a half
un(e) et demi(e)	$1\frac{1}{2}$	one and a half
deux et demi(e)	$2\frac{1}{2}$	two and a half
un tiers	$\frac{1}{3}$	a third
deux tiers	$\frac{2}{3}$	two thirds
un quart	$\frac{1}{4}$	a quarter
trois quarts	$\frac{3}{4}$	three quarters
un sixième	$\frac{1}{6}$	a sixth
trois et cinq sixièmes	$3\frac{5}{6}$	three and five sixths
un douzième	$\frac{1}{12}$	a twelfth
sept douzièmes	$\frac{7}{12}$	seven twelfths
un centième	$\frac{1}{100}$	a hundredth
un millième	$\frac{1}{1000}$	a thousandth

USEFUL PHRASES

une assiette de a plate of
une bande de a group of
beaucoup de lots of
une boîte de a tin *or* can of; a box of
un bol de a bowl of
une bouchée de a mouthful of
un bout de papier a piece of paper
une bouteille de a bottle of
cent grammes de a hundred grammes of
une centaine de (about) a hundred
une cuillerée de a spoonful of
un demi de bière half a litre of beer
une demi-douzaine de half a dozen
un demi-litre de half a litre of
tous (*f* toutes) les deux both of them
une dizaine de (about) ten
une douzaine de a dozen
une foule de loads of
un kilo de a kilo of
à quelques kilomètres de a few kilometres from
un litre de a litre of
une livre de a pound of
un mètre de a metre of

USEFUL PHRASES

à quelques mètres de a few metres from
des milliers de thousands of
la moitié de half of
un morceau de sucre a lump of sugar
un morceau de gâteau a piece of cake
une paire de a pair of
un paquet de a packet of
un peu de a little
une pile de a pile of
la plupart de or **des** most (of)
plusieurs several
une poignée de a handful of
une portion de a portion of
un pot de a pot or tub or jar of
une quantité de a lot of, many
un quart de a quarter of
un tas de a heap of, heaps of
une tasse de a cup of
un tonneau de a barrel of
une tranche de a slice of
trois quarts de three quarters of
un troupeau de a herd of (cattle); a flock of (sheep)
un verre de a glass of

ESSENTIAL WORDS (*masculine*)

le	**bijou** (*pl* -x)	jewel
le	**bracelet**	bracelet
le	**dentifrice**	toothpaste
le	**déodorant**	deodorant
le	**gant de toilette**	face flannel
le	**maquillage**	make-up
le	**miroir**	mirror
le	**parfum**	perfume
le	**peigne**	comb
le	**rasoir**	razor
le	**shampooing** [ʃɑ̃pwɛ̃]	shampoo

USEFUL WORDS (*masculine*)

un	**après-rasage**	after-shave
le	**bigoudi**	curler
le	**blaireau** (*pl* -x)	shaving brush
le	**bouton de manchette**	cufflink
le	**collier**	necklace
le	**démaquillant**	make-up remover
le	**diamant**	diamond
le	**dissolvant**	nail varnish remover
les	**effets personnels**	personal effects
le	**fard**	make-up
le	**fard à paupières**	eye-shadow
le	**fond de teint**	foundation
le	**gel de douche**	shower gel
le	**kleenex**®	tissue
le	**papier hygiénique**	toilet paper
le	**pendentif**	pendant
le	**porte-clefs** (*pl inv*)	key-ring
le	**poudrier**	(powder) compact
le	**rimmel**®	mascara
le	**rouge à lèvres**	lipstick
le	**sèche-cheveux**	hairdryer
le	**vernis à ongles**	nail varnish

ESSENTIAL WORDS (feminine)

la	**bague**	ring
la	**brosse à dents**	toothbrush
la	**chaîne**	chain
la	**chaînette**	chain
la	**crème de beauté**	face cream
la	**crème hydratante**	moisturizer
une	**eau de toilette**	eau de toilette
la	**glace**	mirror
la	**montre**	watch

USEFUL WORDS (feminine)

une	**alliance**	wedding ring
la	**boucle d'oreille** (pl ~s d'oreille)	earring
la	**broche**	brooch
la	**coiffure**	hairstyle
la	**crème à raser**	shaving cream
une	**éponge**	sponge
la	**gourmette**	chain bracelet
la	**manucure**	manicure
la	**mousse à raser**	shaving foam
la	**perle**	pearl
la	**poudre**	face powder
la	**trousse de toilette**	toilet bag

USEFUL PHRASES
se maquiller to put on one's make-up
se démaquiller to take off one's make-up
se coiffer to do one's hair
se peigner to comb one's hair
se raser to shave
se brosser les dents to brush one's teeth

ESSENTIAL WORDS *(masculine)*

un	**arbre**	tree
le	**jardin**	garden
le	**jardinage**	gardening
le	**jardinier**	gardener
les	**légumes**	vegetables
le	**soleil**	sun

IMPORTANT WORDS *(masculine)*

le	**banc**	bench
le	**bouquet de fleurs**	bunch of flowers
le	**buisson**	bush
le	**gazon**	lawn

USEFUL PHRASES

planter to plant
désherber to weed
offrir un bouquet de fleurs à qn to give sb a bunch of flowers
tondre le gazon to mow the lawn
"défense de marcher sur le gazon" "keep off the grass"
mon père aime jardiner my father likes gardening

ESSENTIAL WORDS *(feminine)*

une **abeille**	bee
la **branche**	branch
la **feuille**	leaf
la **fleur**	flower
l'**herbe**	grass
la **pelouse**	lawn
la **plante**	plant
la **pluie**	rain
la **rose**	rose
la **terre**	earth, ground

IMPORTANT WORDS *(feminine)*

la **barrière**	gate; fence
la **culture**	cultivation
la **guêpe**	wasp
les **mauvaises herbes**	weeds
l'**ombre**	shade; shadow
la **plate-bande** (*pl* ~s~s)	flowerbed
la **racine**	root

USEFUL PHRASES

les fleurs poussent the flowers are growing
par terre on the ground
arroser les fleurs to water the flowers
cueillir des fleurs to pick flowers
se mettre à l'ombre to go into the shade
rester à l'ombre to remain in the shade
à l'ombre d'un arbre in the shade of a tree

USEFUL WORDS (*masculine*)

un	**arbuste**	shrub, bush
un	**arrosoir**	watering can
le	**bassin**	(ornamental) pool
le	**bourgeon**	bud
le	**bouton-d'or** (*pl ~s~*)	buttercup
le	**chèvrefeuille**	honeysuckle
le	**chrysanthème**	chrysanthemum
le	**coquelicot**	poppy
le	**crocus**	crocus
le	**feuillage**	leaves
	l'hortensia	hydrangea
le	**jardin potager**	vegetable garden
le	**lierre**	ivy
le	**lilas**	lilac
le	**lis** [lis]	lily
le	**muguet**	lily of the valley
un	**œillet**	carnation
un	**outil**	tool
le	**papillon**	butterfly
le	**parterre**	flowerbed
le	**pavot**	poppy
le	**perce-neige** (*pl inv*)	snowdrop
le	**pissenlit**	dandelion
le	**pois de senteur**	sweet pea
le	**rosier**	rose bush
le	**sol**	earth, soil
le	**tournesol**	sunflower
le	**tronc**	trunk (*of tree*)
le	**tuyau d'arrosage**	hose
le	**ver**	worm
le	**verger**	orchard

USEFUL WORDS (*feminine*)

une	allée	path
la	baie	berry
la	brouette	wheelbarrow
la	clôture	fence
une	épine	thorn
les	graines	seeds
la	:haie	hedge
la	jacinthe	hyacinth
la	jonquille	daffodil
la	marguerite	daisy
une	orchidée	orchid
la	pâquerette	daisy
la	pensée	pansy
la	pivoine	peony
la	primevère	primrose
la	rocaille	rockery
la	rosée	dew
la	serre	greenhouse
la	tige	stalk
la	tondeuse	lawnmower
la	tulipe	tulip
la	violette	violet

ESSENTIAL WORDS (*masculine*)

le	**baigneur**	swimmer
le	**bateau** (*pl* -x) **de pêche**	fishing boat
le	**bikini**	bikini
le	**bord de la mer**	seaside
le	**maillot (de bain)**	swimming trunks *or* swimsuit
le	**pêcheur**	fisherman
le	**pique-nique** (*pl* ~s)	picnic
le	**port**	port, harbour
le	**quai** [ke]	quay
le	**slip de bain**	swimming trunks

IMPORTANT WORDS (*masculine*)

le	**château** (*pl* -x) **de sable**	sandcastle
le	**coup de soleil**	sunburn
le	**crabe**	crab
le	**fond**	bottom
l'	**horizon**	horizon
le	**mal de mer**	seasickness
le	**matelas pneumatique**	airbed, lilo®
le	**sable**	sand
le	**vacancier**	holiday-maker

USEFUL PHRASES

au bord de la mer at the seaside
à l'horizon on the horizon
il a le mal de mer he is sea-sick
nager to swim
se noyer to drown
je vais me baigner I'm going for a swim
plonger dans l'eau to dive into the water
flotter to float

ESSENTIAL WORDS (feminine)

la	**côte**	coast
	l'**eau**	water
une	**île**	island
les	**lunettes de soleil**	sunglasses
la	**mer**	sea
la	**natation**	swimming
la	**pierre**	stone
la	**plage**	beach
la	**promenade**	walk
la	**serviette**	towel

IMPORTANT WORDS (feminine)

la	**chaise longue**	deckchair
la	**crème solaire**	suncream
la	**planche à voile**	windsurfing (board)
la	**traversée**	crossing

USEFUL PHRASES

au fond de la mer at the bottom of the sea
à la plage on the beach; to the beach
faire la traversée en bateau to go across by boat
se bronzer to get a tan
être bronzé(e) to be tanned
il sait nager he can swim

USEFUL WORDS (*masculine*)

	l'**air marin**	sea air
un	**aviron**	oar
le	**bac**	ferry
le	**caillou** (*pl* -x)	pebble
le	**cap** [kap]	headland
le	**coquillage**	shell
le	**courant**	current
un	**équipage**	crew
les	**flots**	waves
le	**gouvernail**	rudder
le	**maître nageur**	lifeguard
le	**marin**	sailor
le	**mât**	mast
le	**matelot**	sailor
le	**naufrage**	shipwreck
les	**naufragés**	people who are shipwrecked
le	**navire**	ship
un	**océan**	ocean
le	**parasol**	parasol
le	**pavillon**	flag
le	**pédalo**	pedalo
le	**phare**	lighthouse
le	**port de plaisance**	marina
le	**radeau** (*pl* -x)	raft
le	**rivage**	shore
le	**rocher**	rock
le	**seau** (*pl* -x)	bucket
le	**vaisseau** (*pl* -x)	vessel

USEFUL WORDS *(feminine)*

les	**algues**	seaweed
une	**ancre**	anchor
la	**baie**	bay
la	**barque**	small boat
la	**bouée**	buoy
la	**cargaison**	cargo
la	**ceinture de sauvetage**	lifebelt
la	**croisière**	cruise
l'	**écume**	foam
une	**embouchure**	mouth *(of river)*
une	**épave**	wreck
la	**falaise**	cliff
une	**insolation**	sunstroke
la	**jetée**	pier
les	**jumelles**	binoculars
la	**marée**	tide
la	**marine**	navy
la	**mouette**	seagull
la	**passerelle**	gangway; bridge *(of ship)*
la	**pelle**	spade
la	**rame**	oar
la	**vague**	wave
la	**voile**	sail; sailing

USEFUL PHRASES

j'ai eu une insolation I had sunstroke
à marée basse/haute at low/high tide
faire de la voile to go sailing

ESSENTIAL WORDS (*masculine*)

un	**achat**	purchase
un	**achat en lignre**	online purchase
	l'argent	money
le	**billet de banque**	banknote
le	**boucher**	butcher
le	**boulanger**	baker
le	**bureau** (*pl* -x) **de poste**	post office
le	**bureau de tabac**	tobacconist's
le	**Caddie®**	trolley
le	**cadeau** (*pl* -x)	present
le	**caissier**	check-out assistant
le	**centime (d'euro)**	euro cent
le	**centre commercial**	shopping centre
le	**charcutier**	pork butcher
le	**chariot**	trolley
le	**chèque**	cheque
le	**chéquier**	cheque book
le	**client**	customer
un	**épicier**	grocer
un	**euro**	euro
le	**fleuriste**	flower shop
le	**franc**	franc
le	**grand magasin**	department store
un	**hypermarché**	supermarket
le	**magasin**	shop
le	**magasin de chaussures**	shoe shop
le	**marché**	market; deal
le	**panier**	basket
le	**prix**	price
le	**rayon**	department
les	**soldes**	sales
le	**souvenir**	souvenir
le	**supermarché**	supermarket
le	**tabac**	tobacconist's
le	**vendeur**	shop assistant, salesman

ESSENTIAL WORDS *(feminine)*

une	**agence de voyages**	travel agent's
	l'**alimentation**	food
la	**banque**	bank
la	**boucherie**	butcher's
la	**boulangerie**	bakery
la	**boutique**	small shop
la	**boutique en ligne**	online shop
la	**caisse**	check-out
la	**caissière**	check-out assistant
la	**carte bancaire**	bank card
la	**Carte bleue®**	debit card
la	**carte de crédit**	credit card
la	**charcuterie**	pork butcher's
la	**cliente**	customer
une	**épicerie**	grocer's
la	**liste**	list
la	**monnaie**	change
la	**parfumerie**	perfume shop/department
la	**pâtisserie**	cake shop
la	**pharmacie**	chemist's
la	**pointure**	(shoe) size
la	**poste**	post office
la	**réduction**	reduction
la	**taille**	size
la	**vendeuse**	shop assistant

USEFUL PHRASES

acheter/vendre to buy/sell
ça coûte combien? how much does this cost?
ça fait combien? how much does that come to?
je l'ai payé(e) 5 euros I paid 5 euros for it
chez le boucher/le boulanger at the butcher's/baker's

IMPORTANT WORDS (*masculine*)

un	**article**	article
le	**coiffeur**	hairdresser
le	**commerçant**	shopkeeper
le	**commerce**	trade
le	**commerce équitable**	fair trade
le	**comptoir**	counter
le	**cordonnier**	cobbler
un	**escalier roulant**	escalator
le	**gérant**	manager
le	**marchand de fruits**	fruiterer
le	**marchand de légumes**	greengrocer
le	**marché aux puces**	flea market
le	**portefeuille**	wallet
le	**porte-monnaie** (*pl inv*)	purse
le	**pressing**	dry-cleaner's
le	**reçu**	receipt
le	**remboursement**	refund
le	**ticket de caisse**	receipt

USEFUL PHRASES

je ne fais que regarder I'm just looking
c'est trop cher it's too expensive
quelque chose de moins cher something cheaper
c'est bon marché it's cheap
"payez à la caisse" "pay at the check-out"
c'est pour offrir? would you like it gift-wrapped?
il doit y avoir une erreur there must be some mistake
la vendeuse m'a fait un paquet-cadeau the shop assistant gift-wrapped
   it for me

IMPORTANT WORDS *(feminine)*

la	**bibliothèque**	library
la	**brocante**	secondhand shop
la	**calculette**	calculator
la	**cordonnerie**	cobbler's
la	**grande surface**	supermarket
la	**librairie**	bookshop
la	**marque**	brand
la	**promotion**	special offer
la	**réclamation**	complaint
la	**vitrine**	shop window

USEFUL PHRASES

avec ça? anything else?

se faire rembourser to get a refund

ce pantalon est trop petit, je voudrais l'échanger these trousers are too small, I'd like to exchange them

créer un compte to create an account

"en vente ici" "on sale here"

une voiture d'occasion a used car

en promotion on special offer

USEFUL WORDS (*masculine*)

un	**agent immobilier**	estate agent
un	**avoir**	credit note
le	**bijoutier**	jeweller
le	**bon cadeau**	gift voucher
le	**coloris**	colour
le	**comparateur**	comparison site
le	**confiseur**	confectioner
un	**horloger**	watchmaker
le	**libraire**	bookseller
le	**magasin de jeux vidéo**	video games shop
le	**marchand de journaux**	newsagent
un	**opticien**	optician
le	**poissonnier**	fishmonger
le	**produit**	product; (*pl*) produce
le	**quincaillier**	ironmonger
le	**rabais**	discount
le	**vidéoclub**	video shop
le	**voyagiste**	travel agent

USEFUL PHRASES

faire du lèche-vitrines to go window shopping
heures d'ouverture opening hours
payer cash to pay cash
payer par carte bancaire to pay by card

USEFUL WORDS *(feminine)*

une	**agence immobilière**	estate agent's
la	**bijouterie**	jeweller's
la	**blanchisserie**	laundry
la	**caisse d'épargne**	savings bank
les	**commissions**	shopping
la	**confiserie**	sweetshop
une	**course**	errand
les	**courses**	shopping
la	**devanture**	shop window; display
la	**droguerie**	hardware shop
une	**encolure**	collar size
une	**horlogerie**	watchmaker's
les	**marchandises**	goods
la	**papeterie**	stationer's
la	**queue** [kø]	queue
la	**quincaillerie**	hardware shop
la	**remise**	discount
la	**succursale**	branch
la	**teinturerie**	dry-cleaner's
la	**vente**	sale

USEFUL PHRASES

en vitrine in the window
faire les courses to go shopping
dépenser to spend

ESSENTIAL WORDS (*masculine*)

le	**badminton**	badminton
le	**ballon**	ball (*large*)
le	**basket**	basketball
le	**billard**	billiards
le	**but** [byt]	goal
le	**champion**	champion
le	**championnat**	championship
le	**cyclisme**	cycling
un	**essai**	try
le	**foot(ball)**	football
le	**golf**	golf
le	**:hand(-ball)**	handball
le	**:hockey**	hockey
le	**jeu** (*pl* -x)	game; play
le	**joueur**	player
le	**match**	match
le	**point**	point
le	**résultat**	result
le	**rugby**	rugby
le	**ski**	skiing; ski
le	**ski nautique**	water skiing
le	**sport**	sport
le	**stade**	stadium
le	**tennis**	tennis; tennis court
le	**terrain**	ground; pitch
le	**volley**	volleyball

USEFUL PHRASES

jouer au football/au tennis to play football/tennis
marquer un but/un point/un essai to score a goal/a point/a try
marquer les points to keep the score
le champion du monde the world champion
gagner/perdre un match to win/lose a match
faire match nul to draw
mon sport préféré my favourite sport

ESSENTIAL WORDS (*feminine*)

	l'aérobic	aerobics
la	balle	ball (*small*)
la	championne	champion
une	équipe	team
	l'équitation	horse-riding
la	gymnastique	gymnastics
la	joueuse	player
la	natation	swimming
la	partie	game
la	piscine	swimming pool
la	planche à voile	windsurfing (board)
la	promenade	walk
la	voile	sailing

USEFUL PHRASES

égaliser to equalize
courir to run
sauter to jump
lancer, jeter to throw
battre qn to beat sb
s'entraîner to train
Liverpool mène (par) 2 à 1 Liverpool is leading by 2 goals to 1
une partie de tennis a game of tennis
il fait partie d'un club he belongs to a club
aller à la piscine to go to the swimming pool
sais-tu nager? can you swim?
faire du sport to do sport
faire une promenade en vélo to go cycling
faire de la voile to go sailing
faire du footing/de l'alpinisme to go jogging/climbing
faire de la marche/de la randonnée to go walking/hiking

USEFUL WORDS (*masculine*)

un	**adversaire**	opponent
	l'**alpinisme**	mountaineering
un	**arbitre**	referee; (*tennis*) umpire
les	**arts martiaux**	martial arts
	l'**athlétisme**	athletics
	l'**aviron**	rowing
le	**catch**	wrestling
le	**champ de course**	race course
le	**championnat**	championship
le	**chronomètre**	stopwatch
le	**débutant**	beginner
le	**détenteur du titre**	titleholder
un	**entraîneur**	trainer, coach
le	**filet**	net
le	**footing**	jogging
le	**gardien de but**	goalkeeper
	l'**hippodrome**	race course
le	**javelot**	javelin
les	**Jeux olympiques**	Olympic Games
le	**jogging**	jogging; tracksuit
le	**judo**	judo
le	**maillot**	(football) jersey
le	**parapente**	paragliding
le	**patin (à glace)**	(ice) skate; (ice) skating
le	**ping-pong**	table tennis
le	**quart de finale**	quarter final
les	**rollers**	roller skates
le	**saut en hauteur**	high jump
le	**saut en longueur**	long jump
le	**score**	score
le	**spectateur**	spectator
le	**squash**	squash
le	**tir**	shooting
le	**tir à l'arc**	archery
le	**toboggan**	toboggan; water slide

IMPORTANT WORDS *(feminine)*

la	**boule**	bowl; billiard ball
les	**boules**	bowls
la	**course**	race
les	**courses**	horse-racing
la	**défense**	defence
	l'**escalade**	climbing
la	**marche**	walking
la	**piste**	ski slope; track
la	**randonnée**	hiking
la	**rencontre**	match

USEFUL WORDS *(feminine)*

les	**baskets**	trainers
la	**boxe**	boxing
la	**compétition**	competition
la	**coupe**	cup
la	**demi-finale**	semi-final
une	**éliminatoire**	heat
	l'**escrime**	fencing
une	**étape**	stage
la	**finale**	final
la	**gagnante**	winner
la	**luge**	sledge; sledging
la	**lutte**	wrestling
la	**mêlée**	scrum
la	**mi-temps** *(pl inv)*	half-time
la	**patinoire**	skating rink
la	**perdante**	loser
la	**plongée**	diving
la	**prolongation**	extra time
la	**raquette**	racket
la	**station de sports d'hiver**	winter sports resort
les	**tennis**	tennis shoes
la	**tribune**	stand

ESSENTIAL WORDS *(masculine)*

un	**acteur**	actor
le	**balcon**	dress circle
le	**billet**	ticket
le	**cinéma**	cinema
le	**cirque**	circus
le	**clip vidéo**	pop video
le	**clown** [klun]	clown
le	**comédien**	actor
le	**comique**	comedian
le	**costume**	costume
le	**film**	film
le	**guichet**	box office
un	**opéra**	opera
un	**orchestre**	orchestra; stalls
le	**programme**	programme
le	**public**	audience
le	**rideau** (*pl* -x)	curtain
le	**spectacle**	show
le	**théâtre**	theatre
le	**western**	western

USEFUL PHRASES

aller au théâtre/au cinéma to go to the theatre/to the cinema
réserver une place to book a seat
un fauteuil d'orchestre a seat in the stalls
mon acteur préféré/actrice préférée my favourite actor/actress
pendant l'entracte during the interval
entrer en scène to come on stage
jouer le rôle de to play the part of

ESSENTIAL WORDS *(feminine)*

une	**actrice**	actress
une	**ambiance**	atmosphere
la	**comédienne**	actress
la	**comique**	comedienne
la	**musique**	music
la	**pièce (de théâtre)**	play
la	**place**	seat
la	**salle**	auditorium; audience
la	**séance**	performance; showing
la	**sortie**	exit
la	**vedette** *(m+f)* **de cinéma**	film star

USEFUL PHRASES

jouer to play
danser to dance
chanter to sing
tourner un film to shoot a film
"prochaine séance: 21 heures" "next showing: 9 o'clock"
"version originale" "in the original language"
"sous-titré" "subtitled"
"complet" "full house"
applaudir to clap
bis! encore!
bravo! bravo!
un film d'amour/de science-fiction a romance/a science fiction film
un film d'adventure/d'horreur an adventure/horror film

IMPORTANT WORDS (*masculine*)

	l'acteur principal	leading man
le	ballet	ballet
un	entracte	interval
le	générique	credits
le	:héros	hero
le	maquillage	make-up
un	ouvreur	usher
le	pourboire	tip
le	sous-titre (*pl ~s*)	subtitle
le	titre	title

USEFUL WORDS (*masculine*)

les	applaudissements	applause
un	auteur dramatique (*m+f*)	playwright
le	décor	scenery
un	écran	screen
le	foyer	foyer
le	metteur en scène	director
le	parterre	stalls
le	personnage	character (*in play*)
le	poulailler	the "gods"
le	producteur	producer
le	projecteur	spotlight
le	réalisateur	director
le	régisseur	stage manager
le	rôle	part
le	scénario	script
le	souffleur	prompter
le	spectateur	member of the audience
le	texte	script, lines
le	vestiaire	cloakroom

IMPORTANT WORDS *(feminine)*

l'**actrice principale**	leading lady
une **affiche**	notice; poster
la **bande-annonce**	trailer
la **comédie**	comedy
la **critique**	review; critics
une **héroïne**	heroine
la **location**	booking; box office
une **ouvreuse**	usherette

USEFUL WORDS *(feminine)*

la **comédie musicale**	musical
la **corbeille**	circle
les **coulisses**	wings
la **distribution**	cast *(on programme)*
une **estrade**	platform
la **farce**	farce
la **fosse d'orchestre**	orchestra pit
une **intrigue**	plot
les **jumelles de théâtre**	opera glasses
la **loge**	box
les **lunettes 3D**	3D glasses
la **metteuse en scène**	director
la **mise en scène**	production
la **première**	first night
la **rampe**	footlights
la **réalisatrice**	director
la **répétition**	rehearsal
la **répétition générale**	dress rehearsal
la **représentation**	performance
la **scène**	stage; scene
la **tragédie**	tragedy

ESSENTIAL WORDS *(masculine)*

un	**an**	year
un	**après-midi** *(pl inv)*	afternoon
un	**instant**	moment
le	**jour**	day
le	**matin**	morning
le	**mois**	month
le	**moment**	moment
le	**quart d'heure**	quarter of an hour
le	**réveil**	alarm clock
le	**siècle**	century
le	**soir**	evening
le	**temps**	time
le	**week-end** *(pl ~s)*	weekend

USEFUL PHRASES

à midi at midday
à minuit at midnight
après-demain the day after tomorrow
aujourd'hui today
avant-hier the day before yesterday
demain tomorrow
hier yesterday
il y a 2 jours 2 days ago
dans 2 jours in 2 days
huit jours a week
quinze jours a fortnight
tous les jours every day
quel jour sommes-nous? what day is it?
le combien sommes-nous? what's the date?
en ce moment at the moment
3 heures moins le quart a quarter to 3
3 heures et quart a quarter past 3
au 21ème siècle in the 21st century
hier soir last night, yesterday evening

ESSENTIAL WORDS (feminine)

une **année**	year
une **après-midi** (pl inv)	afternoon
une **demi-heure** (pl ~s)	half an hour
une **heure**	hour
l'**heure**	time (in general)
la **journée**	day
la **matinée**	morning
la **minute**	minute
la **montre**	watch
la **nuit**	night
la **pendule**	clock
la **quinzaine**	fortnight
la **seconde**	second
la **semaine**	week
la **soirée**	evening

USEFUL PHRASES

l'année dernière/prochaine last/next year

dans une demi-heure in half an hour

une/deux/trois fois once/twice/three times

plusieurs fois several times

3 fois par an 3 times a year

9 fois sur 10 9 times out of 10

il était une fois once upon a time there was

10 à la fois 10 at the same time

quelle heure est-il? what time is it?

avez-vous l'heure? have you got the time?

il est 6 heures/6 heures moins 10/6 heures et demie it is 6 o'clock/10 to 6/ half past 6

il est 14 heures pile it is 2 o'clock exactly

tout à l'heure (past) a short while ago; (future) soon

tôt, de bonne heure early; **tard** late

cette nuit (past) last night; (to come) tonight

IMPORTANT WORDS (*masculine*)

l'**avenir**	future
le **lendemain**	next day
le **retard**	delay; lateness

USEFUL WORDS (*masculine*)

le **cadran**	face (*of clock*)
le **calendrier**	calendar
le **chronomètre**	stopwatch
le **futur**	future; future tense
le **Moyen-Âge**	Middle Ages
le **passé**	past; past tense
le **présent**	present (time); present tense

USEFUL PHRASES

après-demain the day after tomorrow
avant-hier the day before yesterday
le surlendemain two days later
la veille the day before
à l'avenir in the future
un jour de congé a day off
un jour férié a public holiday
un jour ouvrable a weekday
par un jour de pluie on a rainy day
au lever du jour at dawn
le lendemain matin/soir the following morning/evening
à présent now
vous êtes en retard you are late

USEFUL WORDS (*feminine*)

une	**aiguille**	hand (*of clock*)
une	**année bissextile**	leap year
la	**décennie**	decade
une	**époque**	era; time
	l'**horloge**	(large) clock
une	**horloge normande**	grandfather clock

USEFUL PHRASES

vous êtes an avance you are early
cette montre avance/retarde this watch is fast/slow
arriver à temps, arriver à l'heure to arrive on time
combien de temps? how long?
le 3e millénaire the third millennium
faire la grasse matinée to have a lie-in
d'une minute à l'autre any minute now
aujourd'hui en huit a week today
la veille au soir the night before
à cette époque at that time

ESSENTIAL WORDS (*masculine*)

un	**atelier**	workshop
le	**bricolage**	DIY
le	**bricoleur**	handyman
un	**outil**	tool

USEFUL WORDS (*masculine*)

le	**cadenas**	padlock
le	**chantier**	construction site
le	**ciseau** (*pl* -x)	chisel
les	**ciseaux**	scissors
le	**clou**	nail
un	**échafaudage**	scaffolding
un	**élastique**	rubber band
un	**escabeau** (*pl* -x)	stepladder
le	**fil de fer (barbelé)**	(barbed) wire
le	**foret**	drill
le	**marteau** (*pl* -x)	hammer
le	**marteau-piqueur** (*pl* ~x~s)	pneumatic drill
le	**pic**	pickaxe
le	**pinceau** (*pl* -x)	paintbrush
le	**ressort**	spring
le	**scotch**®	Sellotape®
le	**tournevis**	screwdriver

USEFUL PHRASES
faire du bricolage to do odd jobs
enfoncer un clou to hammer in a nail
"attention peinture fraîche" "wet paint"
peindre to paint; **tapisser** to wallpaper

ESSENTIAL WORDS (feminine)

la	**clé, clef**	key; spanner
la	**corde**	rope
la	**machine**	machine

USEFUL WORDS (feminine)

une	**aiguille**	needle
la	**bêche**	spade
la	**boîte à outils**	toolbox
la	**clef anglaise**	spanner
la	**colle**	glue
une	**échelle**	ladder
la	**fourche**	(garden) fork
la	**lime**	file
la	**pelle**	shovel
la	**perceuse**	drill
la	**pile**	battery
les	**pinces**	pliers
la	**pioche**	pickaxe
la	**planche**	plank
la	**punaise**	drawing pin
la	**scie**	saw
la	**serrure**	lock
la	**vis** [vis]	screw

USEFUL PHRASES

"chantier interdit" "construction site: keep out"
pratique handy
couper to cut; **réparer** to mend
visser to screw (in); **dévisser** to unscrew

ESSENTIAL WORDS *(masculine)*

un	**agent (de police)**	policeman
un	**arrêt de bus**	bus stop
le	**bâtiment**	building
le	**bureau** *(pl -x)* **de poste**	post office
le	**bureau** *(pl -x)*	office
le	**centre-ville** *(pl ~s~s)*	town centre
le	**cinéma**	cinema
le	**coin**	corner
le	**commissariat**	police station
les	**environs**	surroundings
un	**habitant**	inhabitant
un	**HLM (habitation à loyer modéré)**	council flat
un	**hôtel**	hotel
un	**hôtel de ville**	town hall
un	**immeuble**	block of flats
le	**jardin public**	park
le	**magasin**	shop
le	**marché**	market
le	**métro**	underground, subway
le	**musée**	museum; art gallery
le	**parc**	park
le	**parking**	car park
le	**piéton**	pedestrian
le	**pont**	bridge
le	**quartier**	district
le	**restaurant**	restaurant
le	**sens interdit**	one-way street
le	**taxi**	taxi
le	**théâtre**	theatre
le	**tour**	tour
le	**touriste**	tourist

ESSENTIAL WORDS (feminine)

une	**auto**	car
la	**banlieue**	suburbs
la	**banque**	bank
la	**boutique**	(small) shop
la	**cathédrale**	cathedral
une	**église**	church
la	**gare**	train station
la	**gare routière**	bus station
une	**HLM (habitation à loyer modéré)**	council flat
la	**laverie automatique**	launderette
la	**mairie**	town hall
la	**piscine**	swimming pool
la	**place**	square
la	**police**	police
la	**pollution**	air pollution
la	**poste**	post office
la	**route**	road
la	**rue**	street
la	**station de taxis**	taxi rank
la	**station-service** (pl ~s~)	petrol station
la	**tour**	tower
une	**usine**	factory
la	**ville**	town, city
la	**voiture**	car
la	**vue**	view

USEFUL PHRASES

je vais en ville I'm going into town
au centre-ville in the town centre
sur la place in the square
une rue à sens unique a one-way street
traverser la rue to cross the street
au coin de la rue at the corner of the street
habiter en banlieue to live in the suburbs

IMPORTANT WORDS *(masculine)*

le	**carnet de tickets**	book of tickets
le	**carrefour**	crossroads
le	**château** *(pl* -x)	castle
le	**DAB (distributeur automatique de billets)**	cashpoint, ATM
un	**embouteillage**	traffic jam
un	**endroit**	place
le	**jardin zoologique**	zoo
le	**kiosque (à journaux)**	newspaper stall
le	**lieu** *(pl* -x)	place
le	**maire**	mayor
le	**monument**	monument
le	**parcmètre**	parking meter
le	**passant**	passer-by
le	**sens unique**	one-way street
le	**temple**	Protestant church
le	**trottoir**	pavement
le	**zoo**	zoo

USEFUL PHRASES

marcher to walk
prendre le bus/le métro to take the bus/the underground
acheter un carnet de tickets to buy a book of 10 tickets
composter to punch (*ticket*)

IMPORTANT WORDS *(feminine)*

une	**affiche**	notice; poster
la	**bibliothèque**	library
la	**chaussée**	road
la	**circulation**	traffic
la	**déviation**	diversion
la	**mosquée**	mosque
la	**rue principale**	main street
la	**synagogue**	synagogue
la	**vieille ville**	old town
la	**zone bleue**	restricted parking zone
la	**zone industrielle**	industrial estate
la	**zone piétonne**	pedestrian precinct

USEFUL PHRASES

industriel(le) industrial
historique historic
joli(e) pretty
laid(e) ugly
propre clean
sale dirty

USEFUL WORDS (*masculine*)

un	**Abribus**®	bus shelter
un	**arrondissement**	district
un	**autobus**	bus
le	**bistrot**	café
le	**bus**	bus
le	**cimetière**	cemetery
le	**citadin**	town dweller
le	**citoyen**	citizen
le	**conseil municipal**	town council
le	**défilé**	parade
un	**édifice**	building
un	**égout**	sewer
le	**faubourg**	suburb
le	**gratte-ciel** (*pl inv*)	skyscraper
le	**panneau** (*pl* -x)	roadsign
le	**passage clouté**	pedestrian crossing
le	**pavé**	cobblestone
le	**refuge**	traffic island
les	**remparts**	ramparts
le	**réverbère**	street lamp
le	**square**	square
le	**virage**	bend

USEFUL WORDS (*feminine*)

une	**agglomération**	built-up area
la	**camionnette de livraison**	delivery van
la	**caserne de pompiers**	fire station
la	**cité universitaire**	halls of residence
les	**curiosités**	sights, places of interest
la	**flèche**	arrow; spire
la	**foule**	crowd
la	**galerie**	art gallery
la	**grand-rue**	main street
une	**impasse**	dead end
la	**piste cyclable**	cycle path
la	**population**	population
la	**poussette**	pushchair
la	**prison**	prison
la	**queue** [kø]	queue
la	**statue**	statue

ESSENTIAL WORDS *(masculine)*

un	**aller-retour**	return ticket
un	**aller simple**	single ticket
les	**bagages**	luggage
le	**billet**	ticket
le	**buffet**	station buffet
le	**compartiment**	compartment
le	**départ**	departure
le	**douanier**	customs officer
le	**frein**	brake
le	**guichet**	ticket office
l'	**horaire**	timetable
le	**mécanicien**	engine-driver
le	**métro**	underground, subway
le	**numéro**	number
les	**objets trouvés**	lost property office
le	**passeport**	passport
le	**plan**	map
le	**pont**	bridge
le	**porteur**	porter
le	**prix du billet**	fare
le	**prix du ticket**	fare
le	**quai** [ke]	platform
les	**renseignements**	information
le	**retard**	delay
le	**sac**	bag
le	**supplément**	extra charge
le	**taxi**	taxi
le	**TGV**	high-speed train
le	**ticket**	ticket
le	**train**	train
le	**train express**	fast train
le	**train rapide**	express train
le	**vélo**	bike
le	**voyage**	journey
le	**voyageur**	traveller

ESSENTIAL WORDS *(feminine)*

une	**arrivée**	arrival
la	**bicyclette**	bicycle
la	**classe**	class
la	**consigne**	left-luggage office
la	**consigne automatique**	left-luggage locker
la	**correspondance**	connection
la	**direction**	direction
la	**douane**	customs
une	**entrée**	entrance
la	**gare**	station
la	**ligne**	line
la	**place**	seat
la	**réduction**	reduction
la	**réservation**	reservation
la	**salle d'attente**	waiting room
la	**sortie**	exit
la	**station de métro**	underground station
la	**station de taxis**	taxi rank
la	**valise**	suitcase
la	**voie**	track, line
la	**voiture**	carriage

USEFUL PHRASES

réserver une place to book a seat
payer un supplément to pay an extra charge
faire/défaire ses bagages to pack/unpack
prendre le train to take the train
manquer son train to miss the train
monter dans le train/bus to get onto the train/bus
descendre du train/bus to get off the train/bus
c'est libre? is this seat free?
composter son billet to punch one's ticket

IMPORTANT WORDS (*masculine*)

le	**chemin de fer**	railway
le	**conducteur**	driver
le	**contrôleur**	ticket collector
un	**escalier roulant**	escalator
le	**pourboire**	tip
le	**tarif**	fare
le	**wagon-lit** (*pl ~s~s*)	sleeping car
le	**wagon-restaurant** (*pl ~s~s*)	dining car

USEFUL WORDS (*masculine*)

le	**chef de gare**	stationmaster
le	**chef de train**	guard
le	**cheminot**	railwayman
le	**coup de sifflet**	whistle
le	**déraillement**	derailment
un	**indicateur**	timetable
le	**passage à niveau**	level crossing
les	**rails**	rails
le	**signal d'alarme**	alarm
le	**train de marchandises**	goods train
le	**trajet**	journey
le	**wagon**	carriage

USEFUL PHRASES

le train est en retard the train is late
un compartiment fumeur/non-fumeur a smoking/non-smoking
  compartment
"défense de se pencher au dehors" "do not lean out of the window"

IMPORTANT WORDS (feminine)

la	**barrière**	barrier
la	**couchette**	sleeping car
la	**destination**	destination
la	**durée**	length (of time)
la	**frontière**	border
la	**portière**	carriage door
la	**SNCF**	French Railways

USEFUL WORDS (feminine)

la	**banquette**	seat
la	**carte d'abonnement**	season ticket
la	**carte jeune**	young persons' discount card
une	**étiquette**	label
la	**locomotive**	locomotive
la	**malle**	trunk
la	**salle d'attente**	waiting room
la	**sonnette d'alarme**	alarm
la	**voie ferrée**	(railway) line or track

USEFUL PHRASES

je t'accompagnerai à la gare I'll go to the station with you
je viendrai te chercher à la gare I'll come and pick you up at the station
le train de 10 heures à destination de Paris/en provenance de Paris
  the 10 o'clock train to/from Paris

ESSENTIAL WORDS (*masculine*)

un **arbre**	tree
le **bois**	wood

USEFUL WORDS (*masculine*)

un **abricotier**	apricot tree
un **arbre fruitier**	fruit tree
le **bouleau** (*pl* -x)	birch
le **bourgeon**	bud
le **buis**	box tree
le **buisson**	bush
le **cerisier**	cherry tree
le **châtaignier**	chestnut tree
le **chêne**	oak
un **érable**	maple
le **feuillage**	foliage
le **figuier**	fig tree
le **frêne**	ash
le **:hêtre**	beech
le **:houx**	holly
un **if**	yew
le **marronnier**	chestnut tree
le **noyer**	walnut tree
un **oranger**	orange tree
un **orme**	elm
le **pêcher**	peach tree
le **peuplier**	poplar
le **pin**	pine
le **platane**	plane tree
le **poirier**	pear tree
le **pommier**	apple tree
le **rameau** (*pl* -x)	branch
le **sapin**	fir tree
le **saule pleureur**	weeping willow
le **tilleul**	lime tree
le **tronc**	trunk
le **verger**	orchard
le **vignoble**	vineyard

ESSENTIAL WORDS (feminine)

la	**branche**	branch
la	**feuille**	leaf
la	**forêt**	forest

USEFUL WORDS (feminine)

	l'**aubépine**	hawthorn
la	**baie**	berry
	l'**écorce**	bark
la	**racine**	root

ESSENTIAL WORDS (*masculine*)

le **champignon**	mushroom
le **chou** (*pl* -x)	cabbage
le **chou-fleur** (*pl* ~x~s)	cauliflower
le **:haricot**	bean
le **:haricot vert**	French bean
les **légumes**	vegetables
un **oignon** [ɔɲɔ̃]	onion
les **petits pois**	peas

USEFUL WORDS (*masculine*)

l'**ail** [aj]	garlic
un **artichaut**	artichoke
le **brocoli**	broccoli
le **céleri**	celery
les **choux de Bruxelles**	Brussels sprouts
le **concombre**	cucumber
le **cresson**	watercress
le **maïs**	corn
les **épinards**	spinach
le **navet**	turnip
le **persil** [pɛrsi]	parsley
le **poireau** (*pl* -x)	leek
le **poivron**	(sweet) pepper
le **radis**	radish

USEFUL PHRASES
cultiver des légumes to grow vegetables
un épi de maïs corn on the cob

ESSENTIAL WORDS *(feminine)*

la	**carotte**	carrot
les	**crudités**	mixed raw vegetables
la	**pomme de terre**	potato
	(pl ~s de terre)	
la	**salade (verte)**	(green) salad
la	**tomate**	tomato

USESFUL WORDS *(feminine)*

les	**asperges**	asparagus
une	**aubergine**	aubergine
la	**betterave**	beetroot
la	**chicorée**	endive
la	**courge**	marrow
la	**courgette**	courgette
une	**endive**	chicory
la	**laitue**	lettuce

USEFUL PHRASES
des carottes râpées grated carrot
biologique organic
végétarien(ne) vegetarian

ESSENTIAL WORDS (*masculine*)

	l'arrière	back
un	autobus	bus
un	autocar	coach
	l'avant	front
un	avion	plane
le	bateau (*pl* -x)	boat
le	bateau à rames/à voile	rowing/sailing boat
le	bus	bus
le	camion	lorry
le	car	coach
le	casque	helmet
le	ferry	ferry
un	hélicoptère	helicopter
un	hovercraft	hovercraft
le	métro	underground
le	mobile home	motorhome
le	moyen de transport	means of transport
le	poids lourd	heavy goods vehicle
le	prix du billet	fare
le	risque	risk
le	scooter	scooter
le	taxi	taxi
le	train	train
les	transports publics	public transport
le	véhicule	vehicle
le	vélo	bike
le	vélomoteur	moped

USEFUL PHRASES
voyager to travel
il est allé à Paris en avion he flew to Paris
prendre le bus/le métro/le train to take the bus/the subway/the train
faire de la bicyclette to go cycling
on peut y aller en voiture you can go there by car

ESSENTIAL WORDS *(feminine)*

la	**bicyclette**	bicycle
la	**camionnette**	van
la	**caravane**	caravan
la	**distance**	distance
la	**moto**	motorbike
la	**voiture**	car

IMPORTANT WORDS *(feminine)*

une	**ambulance**	ambulance
la	**dépanneuse**	breakdown van
la	**voiture de pompiers**	fire engine

USEFUL PHRASES

dépanner qn to repair sb's car
une voiture de location a hire car
une voiture de sport a sports car
une voiture de course a racing car
une voiture de fonction a company car
"voitures d'occasion" "used cars"
démarrer to start, to move off

USEFUL WORDS (*masculine*)

un	**aéroglisseur**	hovercraft
le	**bac**	ferry
le	**bateau-mouche** (*pl* ~x~s)	tour boat in Paris
le	**break** [brɛk]	estate car
le	**bulldozer** [byldozɛʀ]	bulldozer
le	**camion-citerne** (*pl* ~s~s)	tanker
le	**canoë** [kanɔe]	canoe
le	**canot**	rowing boat
le	**canot de sauvetage**	lifeboat
le	**char (d'assaut)**	tank
le	**cyclomoteur**	moped
un	**hydravion**	seaplane
le	**navire**	ship
un	**ovni (objet volant non identifié)**	UFO (unidentified flying object)
le	**paquebot**	passenger liner
le	**pétrolier**	oil tanker (*ship*)
le	**planeur**	glider
le	**porte-avions** (*pl inv*)	aircraft carrier
le	**remorqueur**	tug
le	**semi-remorque** (*pl* ~s)	articulated lorry
le	**sous-marin** (*pl* ~s)	submarine
le	**téléphérique**	cable car
le	**télésiège**	chairlift
le	**tram(way)**	tram
le	**vaisseau** (*pl* -x)	vessel
le	**vélomoteur**	moped
le	**yacht** [jɔt]	yacht

USEFUL WORDS *(feminine)*

la	**camionnette de livraison**	delivery van
la	**charrette**	cart
la	**fusée**	rocket
la	**jeep®**	Jeep®
la	**locomotive**	locomotive
la	**mobylette**	moped
la	**péniche**	barge
la	**remorque**	trailer
la	**soucoupe volante**	flying saucer
la	**vedette**	speedboat

ESSENTIAL WORDS (*masculine*)

l'**air**	air
l'**automne**	autumn
le **brouillard**	fog
le **bulletin de la météo**	weather report
le **ciel**	sky
le **climat**	climate
le **cyclone**	cyclone
le **degré**	degree
l'**est**	east
l'**été**	summer
le **froid**	cold
l'**hiver**	winter
le **nord**	north
le **nuage**	cloud
l'**ouest**	west
le **parapluie**	umbrella
le **printemps**	spring
le **soleil**	sun; sunshine
le **sud**	south
le **temps**	weather
le **tsunami**	tsunami
le **vent**	wind

USEFUL PHRASES

quel temps fait-il? what's the weather like?
il fait chaud/froid it's hot/cold
il fait beau it's a lovely day
il fait mauvais (temps) it's a horrible day
en plein air in the open air
il y a du brouillard it's foggy
30° à l'ombre 30° in the shade
écouter la météo *or* **les prévisions** to listen to the forecast
pleuvoir to rain
neiger to snow
il pleut it's raining
il neige it's snowing

ESSENTIAL WORDS *(feminine)*

la	**glace**	ice
une	**inondation**	flood
la	**météo**	weather forecast
la	**neige**	snow
la	**pluie**	rain
la	**région**	region, area
la	**saison**	season
la	**température**	temperature

USEFUL PHRASES

le soleil brille the sun is shining
le vent souffle the wind is blowing
il gèle it's freezing
geler to freeze
fondre to melt
ensoleillé(e) sunny
orageux(euse) stormy
pluvieux(euse) rainy
frais (fraîche) cool
variable changeable
humide humid
le ciel est couvert the sky is overcast

USEFUL WORDS (*masculine*)

un	**arc-en-ciel** (*pl* arcs-en-ciel)	rainbow
le	**baromètre**	barometer
le	**changement**	change
le	**chasse-neige** (*pl inv*)	snowplough
le	**clair de lune**	moonlight
le	**coucher de soleil**	sunset
le	**courant d'air**	draught
le	**crépuscule**	twilight
le	**dégel**	thaw
le	**déluge**	downpour
un	**éclair**	flash of lightning
le	**flocon de neige**	snowflake
le	**gel**	frost
le	**givre**	frost
le	**glaçon**	icicle
un	**orage**	thunderstorm
un	**ouragan**	hurricane
le	**paratonnerre**	lightning conductor
le	**rayon de soleil**	ray of sunshine
le	**tonnerre**	thunder
le	**verglas**	black ice

IMPORTANT WORDS *(feminine)*

une	**amélioration**	improvement
une	**averse**	shower
la	**chaleur**	heat
une	**éclaircie**	sunny spell
la	**fumée**	smoke
la	**poussière**	dust
les	**précipitations**	rainfall
les	**prévisions (météorologiques)**	(weather) forecast
la	**tempête**	storm
la	**visibilité**	visibility

USEFUL WORDS *(feminine)*

	l'**atmosphère**	atmosphere
	l'**aube**	dawn
la	**brise**	breeze
la	**brume**	mist
la	**canicule**	heatwave
la	**chute de neige**	snowfall
la	**congère**	snowdrift
la	**flaque d'eau**	puddle
la	**foudre**	lightning
la	**gelée**	frost
la	**goutte de pluie**	raindrop
la	**grêle**	hail
une	**inondation**	flood
la	**rafale**	gust of wind
la	**rosée**	dew
la	**sécheresse**	drought
les	**ténèbres**	darkness
la	**vague de chaleur**	heatwave

ESSENTIAL WORDS (*masculine*)

le	**bureau** (*pl* -x)	office
le	**dortoir**	dormitory
le	**drap**	sheet
le	**lit**	bed
les	**lits superposés**	bunk beds
le	**petit déjeuner**	breakfast
le	**repas**	meal
le	**séjour**	stay
le	**silence**	silence
le	**tarif**	rate(s)
le	**visiteur**	visitor
les	**WC**	toilets

IMPORTANT WORDS (*masculine*)

le	**guide**	guidebook
le	**linge**	bedclothes; washing
le	**règlement**	rules
le	**sac à dos**	rucksack
le	**sac de couchage**	sleeping bag

ESSENTIAL WORDS *(feminine)*

une	**AJ**	youth hostel
une	**auberge de jeunesse**	youth hostel
la	**carte**	map; card
la	**cuisine**	kitchen; cooking
la	**douche**	shower
la	**nuit**	night
la	**poubelle**	dustbin
la	**salle à manger**	dining room
la	**salle de bains**	bathroom
la	**salle de jeux**	games room
les	**toilettes**	toilets
les	**vacances**	holidays

IMPORTANT WORDS *(feminine)*

la	**carte d'adhérent**	membership card
la	**randonnée**	hike

USEFUL PHRASES

passer une nuit à l'auberge de jeunesse to spend a night at the youth hostel

je voudrais louer un sac de couchage I would like to hire a sleeping bag

il n'y a plus de place there's no more room

The vocabulary items on pages 204 to 233 have been grouped under parts of speech rather than topics because they can apply in a wide range of circumstances. Use them just as freely as the vocabulary already given.

CONJUNCTIONS

> **What is a conjunction?**
> A **conjunction** is a word such as *and*, *but*, *or*, *so*, *if* and *because*, that links two words or phrases, or two parts of a sentence, for example, *Diane <u>and</u> I have been friends for years; I left <u>because</u> I was bored.*

alors que while
aussi ... que as ... as
avant de + *infinitive* before
car because
cependant however
c'est-à-dire that is to say
comme as
comment how
depuis que since
dès que as soon as
donc so; then
et and
et alors? so what!
lorsque when
maintenant que now (that)
mais but
ne ... que only
ni ... ni neither ... nor

or now
ou or
ou ... ou either ... or
ou bien or
parce que because
pendant que while
pourquoi why
pourvu que + *subj* provided that, so long as
puisque since, because
quand when
que that; than
si if
sinon otherwise
tandis que whilst
tant que so long as
vu que in view of the fact that

ADJECTIVES

> **What is an adjective?**
> An **adjective** is a 'describing' word that tells you more about a person or thing, such as their appearance, colour, size or other qualities, for example, *pretty*, *blue*, *big*.

abordable affordable

abrégé(e) shortened

absurde absurd

accueillant(e) welcoming

actif, active active

actuel(le) present

aérien(ne) aerial

affectueux(euse) affectionate

affreux(euse) dreadful

âgé(e) old

agité(e) restless; stormy (*sea*)

agréable pleasant

agricole agricultural

aigu, aiguë acute; piercing

aimable kind, nice

aîné(e) elder, eldest

amer, amère bitter

amoureux(euse) in love

amusant(e) entertaining

ancien(ne) old, former

animé(e) busy

annuel(le) annual

anonyme anonymous

anxieux(euse) anxious, worried

appliqué(e) diligent

apte capable

arrière: siège *m* **arrière** back seat

assis(e) sitting, seated

aucun(e) no, not any

automatique automatic

autre other

avant: siège *m* **avant** front seat

avantageux(euse) good value

barbu bearded

bas(se) low

beau (bel), belle beautiful

bête silly

bien fine, well; comfortable

bienvenu(e) welcome

bizarre strange, odd

blessé(e) injured

bon(ne) good

bon marché *inv* cheap

bordé(e) de lined with

bouillant(e) boiling

bouleversé(e) upset

bref, brève brief

brillant(e) bright, brilliant; shiny

bruyant(e) noisy

calme calm

capable capable

carré(e) square

catholique Catholic

célèbre famous

certain(e) sure

chaque each

chargé(e) de loaded with; responsible for

charmant(e) delightful
chaud(e) warm, hot
cher, chère dear; expensive
chic smart
choquant(e) shocking
chouette brilliant
chrétien(ne) Christian
clair(e) clear; light
classique classical
climatisé(e) air-conditioned
commode convenient
complet, complète complete; full
compliqué(e) complicated
composé(e) de comprising
compréhensif(ive) understanding
compris(e) understood; included
confortable comfortable
constipé(e) constipated
contemporain(e) contemporary
content(e) happy
continuel(le) continuing
convenable suitable
correct(e) correct
couché(e) lying down
courageux(euse) brave, courageous
court(e) short
couvert(e) de covered with
créé(e) created, established
cruel(le) cruel
cuit(e) cooked
culturel(le) cultural
curieux(euse) curious, strange
dangereux(euse) dangerous
debout standing (up)
décevant(e) disappointing
déchiré(e) torn

découragé(e) discouraged
déçu(e) disappointed
défendu(e) forbidden
dégoûté(e) disgusted
délicat(e) delicate
délicieux(euse) delicious
dernier, dernière last, latest
désagréable unpleasant
désert(e) deserted
désespéré(e) desperate
désolé(e) desolate, sorry
détestable ghastly
détruit(e) destroyed
différent(e) different
difficile difficult
digne worthy
direct(e) direct
disponible available
distingué(e) distinguished
distrait(e) absent-minded
divers(e) different
divertissant(e) entertaining
divin(e) divine
divisé(e) divided
doré(e) golden; gilt
doux, douce gentle; sweet; soft
droit(e) straight; right(hand)
drôle funny
dur(e) hard
économique economic; economical
effrayé(e) frightened
égal(e) equal; even
électrique electric
élégant(e) elegant
élevé(e) high; **bien élevé(e)** well-mannered
embêtant(e) annoying

enchanté(e) delighted
énervé(e) irritated; nervous
ennuyé(e) bothered
ennuyeux(euse) boring
énorme huge
ensoleillé(e) sunny
entendu(e) agreed
entier, entière whole
épais(se) thick
épouvantable terrible
épuisé(e) exhausted
essentiel(le) essential
essoufflé(e) out of breath
étendu(e) stretched out
étonnant(e) astonishing
étonné(e) astonished
étrange strange
étranger, étrangère foreign
étroit(e) narrow
éveillé(e) awake
évident(e) obvious
exact(e) exact
excellent(e) excellent
expérimenté(e) experienced
extraordinaire extraordinary
fâché(e) angry
facile easy
faible weak
fatigant(e) tiring
fatigué(e) tired
faux, fausse false, wrong
favori(te) favourite
fermé(e) closed
féroce fierce
fier, fière proud
fin(e) fine; thin

final(e) final
fondé(e) founded
formidable tremendous
fort(e) strong; hard
fou, folle mad
fragile fragile; frail
frais, fraîche fresh, cool
froid(e) cold
furieux(euse) furious
futur(e) future
gai(e) cheerful
gauche left(hand)
général(e) general
généreux(euse) generous
génial(e) brilliant
gentil(le) kind, nice
gonflé(e) swollen
gracieux(euse) graceful
grand(e) big; tall
gratuit(e) free
grave serious
gros(se) big; fat
habile skilful
habitué(e) à used to
habituel(le) usual
haut(e) high; tall
heureux(euse) happy
historique historical
honnête honest
identique identical
illuminé(e) lit; floodlit
illustré(e) illustrated
imaginaire imaginary
immense huge
immobile motionless
important(e) important

impossible impossible
impressionnant(e) impressive
imprévu(e) unforeseen
inattendu(e) unexpected
incapable (de) incapable (of)
inconnu(e) unknown
incroyable unbelievable
indispensable indispensable
industriel(le) industrial
inondé(e) flooded
inquiet, inquiète worried
insouciant(e) carefree
insupportable unbearable
intelligent(e) intelligent
interdit(e) prohibited
intéressant(e) interesting
interminable endless
international(e) international
interrompu(e) interrupted
inutile useless
irrité(e) annoyed
isolé(e) isolated
jeune young
jaloux(ouse) jealous
joli(e) pretty
joyeux(euse) merry, cheerful
juif, juive Jewish
juste just; correct
lâche cowardly
laid(e) ugly
large wide; broad
léger, légère light
lent(e) slow
leur/leurs their
libre free
local(e) local

long(ue) long
lourd(e) heavy
magique magical
magnifique magnificent
maigre thin
malade ill
malheureux(euse) unhappy, unfortunate
malhonnête dishonest
mauvais(e) bad
mécanique mechanical
méchant(e) naughty
mécontent(e) unhappy
médical(e) medical
meilleur(e) better, best
même same
merveilleux(euse) marvellous
militaire military
minable pathetic
mince slim
mobile mobile; moving; movable
moche ugly
moderne modern
moindre least
mon/ma/mes my
montagneux(euse) mountainous
mort(e) dead
mouillé(e) wet
mouvementé(e) lively
moyen(ne) average
mû, mue (par) moved (by)
multicolore multicoloured
muni(e) de provided with
municipal(e) municipal, town
mûr(e) ripe
musclé(e) muscular
musical(e) musical

musulman(e) Muslim
mystérieux(euse) mysterious
natal(e) native
national(e) national
naturel(le) natural
né(e) born
nécessaire necessary
négatif(ive) negative
nerveux(euse) nervous
net(te) clear
neuf, neuve new
nombreux(euse) numerous
normal(e) normal
notre/nos our
nouveau (nouvel), nouvelle new
noyé(e) drowned
obligatoire compulsory
obligé(e) de obliged to
occupé(e) taken; busy; engaged
officiel(le) official
ordinaire ordinary
original(e) original
orné(e) de decorated with
outré(e) outraged
ouvert(e) open
paisible peaceful
pâle pale
pareil(le) similar, same
paresseux(euse) lazy
parfait(e) perfect
particulier, particulière particular; private
passionnant(e) exciting
passionné(e) passionate
patient(e) patient
pauvre poor
pénible painful

permanent(e) permanent
perpétuel(le) perpetual
personnel(le) personal
petit(e) small, little
pittoresque picturesque
plat(e) flat
plein(e) (de) full (of)
plusieurs several
pneumatique inflatable
poli(e) polite; polished
populaire popular
portatif(ive) portable
positif(ive) positive
possible possible
pratique practical; handy
précédent(e) previous
précieux(euse) precious
précis(e) precise
préféré(e) favourite
premier, première first
pressant(e) urgent
pressé(e): être pressé(e) to be in a hurry
prêt(e) ready
primaire primary
privé(e) private
privilégié(e) privileged
prochain(e) next
proche nearby; close
profond(e) deep
propre own; clean
protestant(e) Protestant
prudent(e) cautious
public, publique public
publicitaire publicity
quel(le) what
quelque(s) some

rafraîchissant(e) refreshing
rangé(e): bien rangé(e) neat and tidy
rapide fast
rare rare
ravi(e) delighted
récent(e) recent
reconnaissant(e) grateful
rectangulaire rectangular
réel(le) real
religieux(euse) religious
réservé(e) reserved
responsable (de) responsible (for)
rêveur(euse) dreamy
riche rich
ridicule ridiculous
rond(e) round
rusé(e) cunning
sage well-behaved; wise
sain et sauf safe and sound
sale dirty
sanitaire sanitary
satisfait(e) (de) satisfied (with)
sauvage wild
scolaire school (*year etc*)
sec, sèche dry
second(e) second
secondaire secondary
secret, secrète secret
semblable similar
sensible sensitive
sérieux(euse) serious
serré(e) tight
seul(e) alone
sévère severe
simple simple
sincère sincere

sinistre sinister
situé(e) situated
social(e) social
solennel(le) solemn
solide solid
sombre dark
son/sa/ses his, her, its, one's
soudain(e) sudden
souriant(e) smiling
sous-marin(e) underwater
spécial(e) special
suivant(e) following
suivi(e) de followed by
super super
superbe magnificent
supérieur(e) upper; advanced
supplémentaire extra
sûr(e) sure
surprenant(e) surprising
sympa(thique) nice, likeable
technique technical
tel(le) such
temporaire temporary
terrible terrible
théâtral(e) theatrical
tiède lukewarm
timide shy
ton/ta/tes your
touristique tourist (*area etc*)
tout/toute/toutes all
traditionnel(le) traditional
tranquille quiet, peaceful
trempé(e) soaked
triste sad
troublé(e) disturbed
typique typical

uni(e) plain
unique only; unique
urbain(e) urban
urgent(e) urgent
utile useful
valable valid
varié(e) varied; various
vaste vast
véritable real

vide empty
vieux (vieil), vieille old
vif, vive bright
vilain(e) naughty; ugly; nasty
violent(e) violent
vivant(e) alive; lively
voisin(e) neighbouring
votre/vos your
vrai(e) real, true

ADVERBS AND PREPOSITIONS

What is an adverb?
An **adverb** is a word used with verbs to give information on where, when or how an action takes place, for example, *here, today, quickly*. An adverb can also add information to adjectives and other adverbs, for example, *extremely quick, very quickly*.

What is a preposition?
A **preposition** is one word such as *at, for, with, into* or *from*, or words such as *in front of* or *near to*, which are usually followed by a noun or a pronoun.

Prepositions show how people and things relate to the rest of the sentence, for example, *She's at home; It's for you; You'll get into trouble; It's in front of you*.

à to, at
abord: d'abord first, at first;
  tout d'abord first of all;
  aux abords de alongside
absolument absolutely
actuellement at present
admirablement admirably
afin de so as to
ailleurs elsewhere;
  d'ailleurs moreover
ainsi thus;
  ainsi que as well as
alors then
anxieusement anxiously
après after;
  après-demain the day after tomorrow;
  d'après according to
assez fairly, quite;

assez de enough
aujourd'hui today
auparavant previously
auprès de next to
aussi also, too; as
aussitôt at once
autant (de) as much; as many;
  d'autant plus (que) all the more (since)
autour (de) around
autrefois formerly
autrement otherwise; differently;
  autrement dit in other words;
autrement que other than
avance: à l'avance in advance;
  d'avance in advance
avant (de) before
avec with
bas: en bas downstairs, at the bottom

beaucoup a lot; much;
  beaucoup de a lot of; many
bien well;
  bien entendu of course
bientôt soon
bord: à bord (de) on board;
  au bord de beside
bout: au bout de after; at the end of
bref in short
brusquement suddenly
cependant however
certainement certainly
chez at (or to) the house;
  chez moi/toi/lui/elle
  at my/your/his/her house
combien (de) how much,
  how many
comme as, like;
  comme d'habitude as usual;
  comme toujours as usual
comment how
complètement completely
compris: y compris including
conséquent: par conséquent
  as a result
continuellement continually
contraire: au contraire on the
  contrary
contre against;
  ci-contre opposite;
  par contre on the other hand
côté: à côté de next to, beside;
  de ce côté (de) on this side (of);
  de l'autre côté (de) on the other
  side (of);
  juste à côté next door
couramment fluently
cours: au cours de during

dans in, into
davantage (de) more
de of, from
debout standing
dedans inside
dehors outside
déjà already
demain tomorrow;
  après-demain the day after
  tomorrow
depuis since, for
derrière behind
dès from; **dès que** as soon as
dessous underneath;
  ci-dessous below;
  en dessous (de) below
dessus on top;
  au-dessus (de) above;
  ci-dessus above
devant in front (of)
doucement gently
droit: tout droit straight (on)
droite: à droite on the right,
  to the right
dur hard
effet: en effet indeed
également also; equally
encore still; again;
  encore une fois once again
enfin at last
énormément (de) a lot (of)
ensemble together
ensuite then
entièrement entirely
entre between
environ about
éventuellement possibly

évidemment obviously
exactement exactly
exprès on purpose
extérieur: à l'extérieur (de) outside
extrêmement extremely
face à faced with;
  en face (de) opposite
facilement easily
façon: de façon à so as to
fidèlement faithfully
finalement in the end; after all
fort hard
franchement frankly
gauche: à gauche on the left,
  to the left
général: en général usually
généralement generally
gentiment nicely
grâce à thanks to
gravement gravely; seriously
guère: ne ... guère hardly
habitude: d'habitude usually;
  comme d'habitude as usual
hasard: par hasard by chance;
  au hasard at random
haut: en haut (de) at the top (of);
  de haut en bas from top to bottom
heure: à l'heure on time;
  de bonne heure early
heureusement fortunately
hier yesterday;
  avant-hier the day before
  yesterday
ici here
immédiatement immediately
importe: n'importe où anywhere
intellectuellement intellectually

intérieur: à l'intérieur (de) inside
jadis formerly, once
jamais ever;
  ne ... jamais never
jusque: jusqu'à until;
  jusqu'ici so far, until now;
  jusque-là until then
justement exactly
là there; **là-bas** over there;
  là-haut up there
légèrement slightly
lendemain:
  le lendemain the next day;
  le lendemain matin the next
  morning
lentement slowly
loin (de) far (from)
long: le long de along
longtemps for a long time
lourdement heavily
maintenant now
mal badly
malgré in spite of
malheureusement unfortunately
manuellement manually
maximum: au maximum
  at the maximum
même same; even;
  même pas not even;
  quand même even so
mentalement mentally
mieux better; **le mieux** best
milieu: au milieu de in the middle of
moins less, minus;
  moins de less than, fewer than;
  au moins at least;
  du moins at least

mystérieusement mysteriously
naturellement of course, naturally
nerveusement nervously
normalement normally
notamment especially
nouveau: de nouveau again
nulle part nowhere
ne ... nullement in no way
où where;
  n'importe où anywhere
outre: en outre furthermore
paisiblement peacefully
par by; through;
  par terre on the ground;
  par-dessous under;
  par-dessus over
parfaitement perfectly
parfois sometimes
parmi among
part: à part apart (from);
  nulle part nowhere;
  quelque part somewhere
particulier: en particulier
  in particular
particulièrement particularly
partiellement partially
partir: à partir de from
partout everywhere
pas: pas du tout not at all;
  pas loin de not far from;
  pas mal de a lot of
patiemment patiently
peine: à peine scarcely, hardly,
  barely
pendant during, for
peu: peu à peu little by little;
  à peu près about, approximately

peut-être perhaps, maybe
poliment politely
plus [plys]:
  deux plus deux two plus two;
  en plus moreover;
  de plus moreover;
  de plus en plus [dəplyzɑ̃ply]
    more and more;
plus [ply]:
  plus de (pommes) no more
    (apples);
  plus de (dix) more than (ten);
  ne ... plus no more, no longer;
  plus tard later;
  non plus neither, either;
  moi non plus! nor me!
plutôt rather
pour for; in order to
pourtant yet, nevertheless
près de near
présent: à présent at present
presque almost, nearly
proximité: à proximité de
  near to
puis then
quand when;
  quand même however, even so,
    nevertheless
quant à (moi) as for (me)
quelquefois sometimes
quelque part somewhere
rapidement quickly
rarement rarely
récemment recently
régulièrement regularly
retard: en retard late
sans without;
  sans cesse incessantly

sauf except
selon according to
sérieusement seriously
seulement only
simplement simply
soigneusement carefully
soudain suddenly
sous under
souvent often
sur on
sûrement certainly
sur-le-champ at once
surtout especially
tant de so much, so many
tard late;
  plus tard later;
  trop tard too late
tellement so; so much
temps: de temps en temps from time to time;
  de temps à autre from time to time;

en même temps at the same time
tôt early;
  trop tôt too soon, too early;
  le plus tôt possible as soon as possible
toujours always; still
tout: en tout in all;
  tout d'abord first of all;
  tout à coup suddenly;
  tout à fait completely, quite;
  tout près (de) very near;
  tout de suite at once
travers: à travers through
très very
trop too; too much;
  trop de too much, too many
uniquement only
un à un one by one
vers towards; about (of time)
vite quickly, fast
vraiment really
y there, to that place, in that place

SOME EXTRA NOUNS

> **What is a noun?**
> A **noun** is a naming word for a living being, a thing, or an idea,
> for example, *woman, Andrew, desk, happiness.*

un **accent** accent
un **accord** agreement
un **accueil** reception
une **action** action
une **activité** activity
les **affaires** *fpl* things
l'**âge** *m* age
l'**air** *m* air
une **ambition** ambition
une **âme** soul
un **ami** friend
une **amie** friend
l'**amour** *m* love
l'**angoisse** *f* anguish, distress
une **annonce** advertisement
une **antenne parabolique**
    satellite dish
l'**argent** *m* silver; money
l'**arrière** *m* back, rear
un **article** article
l'**attention** *f* attention;
    à l'attention de for the attention of
un **attrait** attraction
un **avantage** advantage
une **aventure** adventure
un **avis** notice; opinion;
    à mon avis in my opinion
le **bain** bath
la **barrière** gate; fence
la **bataille** battle

le **bâton** stick
la **beauté** beauty
la **bêtise** stupidity
le **bien** good
la **bise** kiss
le **bonheur** happiness
le **bonhomme de neige** snowman
la **boue** mud
la **bousculade** bustle
le **bout** end
le **bruit** noise
le **but** aim; goal
le **calme** peace, calm
le **candidat** candidate
le **canif** penknife
le **caractère** character, nature
la **carte d'identité** ID card
le **cas** case; **en cas de** in case of;
    en tout cas in any case
la **catastrophe** disaster
le/la **catholique** Catholic
la **cause** cause;
    à cause de because of
le **CD-ROM** CD-ROM
le **centimètre** centimetre
le **centre** centre
le **cercle** circle
le **chagrin** distress
la **chance** luck
la **chapelle** chapel

le **chapitre** chapter
le **charme** charm
le **chef** boss
le **chiffre** figure
le **choix** choice
la **chose** thing
le/la **chrétien(ne)** Christian
le **chuchotement** whispering
la **civilisation** civilization
le **classement** classification
la **cloche** bell
le **clocher** steeple
le **coin** corner
la **colère** anger
la **colonne** column
le **commencement** beginning
la **compagne** companion; partner
le **compagnon** companion; partner
la **comparaison** comparison
le **compte** calculation
la **confiance** confidence
le **confort** comfort
la **conscience** conscience
le **conseil** advice
la **construction** construction
le **contraire** the opposite
la **copie** copy
la **corbeille** basket
la **corde** rope
le **correcteur orthographique**
  spellchecker
le/la **correspondant(e)**
  correspondent
le **côté** side
le **coup** blow, bang, knock
le **courage** courage, bravery
le **cours** course, lesson

la **coutume** custom
le **couvent** convent
la **crainte** fear
le **cri** cry
la **croix** cross
la **cuisine** kitchen; cookery
la **culture** culture
le **curé** vicar, priest
la **curiosité** curiosity
le **danger** danger
les **débris** *mpl* wreckage
le **début** beginning
la **décision** decision
les **dégâts** *mpl* damage
le **délai** time limit
le **déodorant** deodorant
le **désarmement** disarmament
le **désastre** disaster
le **désir** wish
le **désordre** disorder
le **destin** destiny
le **détail** detail
la **détresse** distress
Dieu God
la **différence** difference;
  **quelle est la différence
  entre X et Y?** what is the difference
  between X and Y?
la **difficulté** difficulty
la **dimension** dimension
la **direction** direction
la **discipline** discipline
la **dispute** argument
le **disque dur** hard disk
la **distance** distance
le **distributeur** dispenser
le **documentaire** documentary

la documentation documentation
le doute doubt;
  sans doute no doubt; probably
le drapeau flag
le droit right
la droite the right
la durée time
un échange exchange;
  en échange de in exchange for
une échelle ladder
l'économie f economy; saving
un effet effect
un effort effort
un électeur elector
une élection election
l'élégance f elegance
un endroit place
l'énergie f energy
l'enfance f childhood
un ennemi enemy
l'ennui m boredom; problem
une enseigne sign
un ensemble group
l'enthousiasme m enthusiasm
un entretien conversation;
  interview
les environs mpl surrounding
  district
l'épaisseur f thickness
une erreur mistake
l'espace m space
une espèce sort; species;
  en espèces in cash
un espoir hope
l'essentiel m the main thing
une étape stage; stopping point
un état state

l'étendue f extent
une étoile star
l'étonnement m astonishment
un événement event
un excès excess
un exemple example;
  par exemple for example
l'exil m exile
une expérience experience;
  experiment
un expert expert
une explication explanation
une exposition exhibition
un extrait extract
la fabrication manufacture
la façon way;
  de cette façon in this way
le fait fact
la famille family
la fanfare brass band; fanfare
la faute fault;
  c'est de ma faute it's my fault
la fermeture closure
le feu fire
la fin end
la flèche arrow
la foi faith
la fois time
la folie madness
le fond background; bottom
la force strength
la forme shape
la foule crowd
la fraîcheur freshness
les frais mpl expenses
le franc franc
la gaieté, la gaîté gaiety

la gauche the left
le genre type, kind, sort
la gentillesse kindness
le goût taste; **chacun ses goûts**
  each to his own
le gouvernement government
la grandeur size
le gros lot first prize
le groupe group
la guerre war
le guide guide
l'habileté f skill
une habitude habit
l'harmonie f harmony
le :haut-parleur
  (pl haut-parleurs) loudspeaker
la :hauteur height
l'honneur m honour
les honoraires mpl fees
la :honte shame
l'humeur f mood
l'humour m humour
l'hygiène f hygiene
une idée idea
un/une idiot(e) idiot
une image picture
l'imagination f imagination
un/une imbécile idiot
un/une immigré(e) immigrant
l'importance f importance
un/une inconnu(e) stranger
un inconvénient disadvantage
les informations fpl news
un inspecteur inspector
les instructions fpl instructions
l'intérêt m interest
une interruption break, interruption

une interview interview
une invitation invitation
la jalousie jealousy
la joie joy
le jouet toy
le jour day
le journal (pl journaux) newspaper
le/la juif/juive Jew
la largeur width
la larme tear
le lecteur reader
le lecteur de disquettes disk drive
la légende legend, caption
le lever de soleil sunrise
le lieu place;
  au lieu de instead of
la ligne line
la limite boundary, limit
la liste list
la littérature literature
la livre (sterling) pound (sterling)
la location rental
le loisir leisure
la longueur length
la Loterie nationale National
  Lottery
la lumière light
la lune moon
la lutte struggle
le machin thing, contraption
le magazine magazine
la malchance bad luck
le malheur misfortune
la manière way
le manque (de) lack (of)
le matériel hardware
le maximum maximum

la médecine medicine (*science*)
le mélange mixture
le membre member
la mémoire memory
le mensonge lie
la messe mass
la méthode method
le mieux best
le milieu middle
le minimum minimum
le Ministère de the Ministry of
le mot word; message
le moyen (de) the means (of);
  au moyen de by means of
le/la musulman(e) Muslim
le mystère mystery
le niveau (*pl* -x) level
le nom name
le nombre number
la nourriture food
la nouvelle (piece of) news
un objet object
l'obscurité *f* darkness
une observation remark
une occasion opportunity; occasion
un octet byte
une œuvre work
une ombre shadow
une opinion opinion
un ordre order
l'orgueil *m* pride
l'ouverture *f* opening
la page page
la paire pair
la paix peace
le panier basket

le panneau (*pl* -x) sign, notice
le pari bet
la parole word
la part part; **de la part de** from
la partie part
le pas footstep
la patience patience
le pays country
la peine difficulty; sentence
la pensée thought
la permission permission
la perruque wig
la personne person
le pétrole oil, petroleum;
  paraffin
le peuple nation
la phrase sentence
la pile battery
la plaisanterie joke
le plaisir pleasure
le plan plan; map;
  au premier plan in the
  foreground;
  à l'arrière plan in the background
le plateau (*pl* -x) tray; plateau
la plupart de most (of)
le poids weight
le point point, mark; full stop
le point de vue point of view
la politesse politeness
la politique politics
le pont bridge, deck
portée: à portée de la main
  within arm's reach
le portrait portrait
la position position

la **possibilité** possibility, opportunity
la **poupée** doll
la **poussière** dust
le **pouvoir** power
les **préparatifs** *mpl* preparations
la **préparation** préparation
la **présence** presence
le **pressentiment** feeling
le **principe** principle;
 en **principe** in principle
le **problème** problem
le **produit** product; produce
la **profondeur** depth
le **projet** plan
la **propreté** cleanliness
la **prospérité** prosperity
les **provisions** provisions
la **prudence** caution
la **publicité** publicity
la **qualité** quality
la **question** question
la **queue** tail
le **raccourci** short cut
la **raison** reason
le **rapport** connection
la **reine** queen
la **religion** religion
les **remerciements** *mpl* thanks
le **remue-ménage** commotion
la **rencontre** meeting
le **rendez-vous** appointment
les **renseignements** *mpl*
 information
la **réponse** reply
la **reprise** resumption
la **réputation** reputation

le **rescapé** survivor
le **réseau** (*pl* -x) network
la **résolution** resolution
le **respect** respect
les **restes** *mpl* remains
le **résultat** result
le **résumé** summary
le **retour** return;
 de **retour** back
la **réussite** success
le **rêve** dream
la **révolution** revolution
le **roi** king
le **ruisseau** stream
le **rythme** rhythm
la **saleté** dirtiness
le **salon de beauté** beauty parlour
le **sang-froid** calm
le **sanglot** sob
le **schéma** diagram
le **seau** bucket
le **secours** help
le **secret** secret
la **section** section
la **sécurité** security
le **séjour** stay
la **sélection** selection
la **semaine** week
le **sens** sense
la **sensation** feeling
la **série** series
le **service** service;
 de **service** on duty
le **signe** sign
le **silence** silence
la **situation** situation
la **société** society

la solution solution
la somme sum
le son sound
le sort fate
la sorte sort, kind
le soupçon suspicion
le sourire smile
le souvenir souvenir; memory
le spectateur spectator
le/la stagiaire trainee
le style style
le succès success
la sueur sweat
le sujet subject;
  au sujet de about
la surprise surprise
la surveillance supervision; watch
le système system
la tache stain
la tâche task
le talent talent
le tas heap, pile
le taux de change exchange rate
la taxe tax
le téléscope telescope
le/la téléspectateur(trice) viewer
la tentative attempt

le terme term, expression
le texte text
la théorie theory
la timidité shyness
le tour turn; trick; **c'est ton tour**
  it's your turn
le tournoi tournament
la tragédie tragedy
le traitement treatment; salary
le tremblement de terre
  earthquake
la tristesse sadness
le tube tube; hit song
le type type; guy
le va-et-vient comings and goings
la valeur value
la vapeur steam
la veine luck
la version version
le verso back (of page)
la victoire victory
la vie life
les vœux *mpl* wishes
le voyage journey
la vue view; **de vue** by sight;
  en vue de with a view to

VERBS

> **What is a verb?**
> A **verb** is a 'doing' word which describes what somebody or something does, what they are, or what happens to them, for example, *play, be, disappear.*

abandonner to abandon

abîmer to spoil, to damage

aboutir to end

s'abriter to shelter

accepter to accept

accompagner to go with

accomplir to accomplish

s'accoutumer à to become accustomed to

accrocher to hang (up); to catch (à on)

accueillir to welcome

accuser to accuse

acheter to buy

achever to finish

admettre to admit

admirer to admire

adorer to adore

s'adresser à to apply to; to speak to

afficher to display

affirmer to maintain, to assert

agacer to irritate

agir to act, to behave;
  il s'agit de it is a question of

s'agrandir to grow

aider qn à to help sb to

aimer to like, to love;
  aimer bien to like;
  aimer mieux to prefer

ajouter to add

aller to go;
  aller chercher qn to go and meet sb;
  s'en aller to go away

allumer to switch on; to light

amener to bring

s'amuser to enjoy oneself

annoncer to announce

annuler to cancel

s'apercevoir de to notice

appartenir (à) to belong (to)

appeler to call;
  s'appeler to be called

apporter to bring

apprécier to appreciate

apprendre (à faire qch) to learn (to do sth);
  apprendre qch à qn to teach sb sth

s'approcher de to approach

approuver to approve

appuyer to press;
  s'appuyer to lean

arracher to pull out; to snatch; to tear

s'arranger: cela s'arrangera it will be all right

arrêter to stop; to arrest;
  s'arrêter to stop

arriver to arrive; to happen

s'asseoir to sit down

assister à to attend, to be present at, to go to

assurer to assure; to insure

attacher to tie, to fasten

attaquer to attack

atteindre to reach

attendre to wait (for)

attirer to attract

attraper to catch

augmenter to increase

(s')avancer to go forward

avoir to have;
 avoir l'air to seem;
 avoir besoin de to need;
 avoir chaud/froid to be hot/cold;
 avoir envie de to want to; **avoir l'habitude de** to be in the habit of;
 avoir honte (de) to be ashamed (of);
 avoir l'intention de to intend to;
 avoir lieu to take place;
 avoir du mal à to have difficulty in;
 en avoir marre to be fed up;
 avoir peur to be afraid;
 avoir raison/tort to be right/wrong

avouer to confess

baisser to lower

balbutier to stammer

barrer to block

bâtir to build

battre to beat;
 se battre to fight

bavarder to chat

bloquer to block

bouger to move

bouleverser to upset

bricoler to potter about, to do odd jobs

briller to shine

briser to break

brûler to burn

(se) cacher to hide

(se) calmer to calm down

casser to break

causer to cause; to chat

cesser (de) to stop

changer to change;
 changer d'avis to change one's mind

chanter to sing

charger to load

chasser to chase (off); to get rid of

chauffer to heat up

chercher to look for

choisir to choose

chuchoter to whisper

circuler to move

cirer to polish

cocher to tick

collaborer to collaborate

collectionner to collect

coller to stick

commander to order

commencer (à) to begin (to)

compenser to compensate for

comporter to comprise

composer to compose; to make up; to dial

composter to date-stamp; to punch

comprendre to understand

compter to count; to intend to

concerner to concern

conclure to conclude

condamner to condemn;
  to sentence
conduire to drive;
  se conduire to behave
confectionner to make
confirmer to confirm
connaître to know
consacrer to devote
conseiller to advise
conserver to keep
considérer to consider
consister to consist
consommer to consume
constater to establish
constituer to make up
construire to build
consulter to consult
contacter to get in touch with
contempler to contemplate
contenir to contain
continuer to continue
convenir to be suitable
copier to copy
corriger to correct
se coucher to go to bed;
  to lie down
coudre to sew
couler to flow
couper to cut (off)
courir to run
coûter to cost
couvrir to cover
craindre to fear
créer to create
creuser to dig
crier to shout
critiquer to criticize

croire to believe
cueillir to pick
cultiver to grow
danser to dance
se débrouiller to manage
décevoir to disappoint
déchirer to tear
décider (de) to decide (to);
  se décider (à) to make up one's
  mind (to)
déclarer to declare
découper to cut up
se décourager to become
  discouraged
découvrir to discover
décrire to describe
défendre to forbid; to defend
dégager to clear
se déguiser to dress up
demander to ask;
  demander à qn de faire qch to ask
  sb to do sth;
  se demander to wonder
demeurer to live
démolir to demolish
dépasser to overtake
se dépêcher to hurry
dépendre de to depend on
déplaire: cela me déplaît
  I don't like it
déposer to put down
déranger to disturb
désapprouver to disapprove of
descendre to come or go down;
  to get off; to take down
déshabiller to undress
désirer to desire, to want

désobéir to disobey
dessiner to draw
détester to hate
détourner to divert
détruire to destroy
développer to develop
devenir to become
deviner to guess
devoir to have to (*must*)
différer (de) to be different (from)
diminuer to reduce
dire to say, to tell
diriger to direct;
  se diriger vers to go towards
discuter to discuss
disparaître to disappear
se disputer to argue
distinguer to distinguish
distribuer to distribute
diviser to divide
dominer to dominate
donner to give
donner sur to overlook
dormir to sleep
se doucher to have a shower
douter (de) to doubt
dresser to set up;
  se dresser to stand (up)
durer to last
échanger to exchange
s'échapper (de) to escape (from)
éclairer to light (up)
éclater de rire to burst out laughing
économiser to save
écouter to listen (to)
écraser to crush;
  s'écraser to crash

s'écrier to cry out
écrire to write;
  s'écrire to write to each other;
  ça s'écrit comment? how do you spell it?
effacer to erase
effectuer to carry out
effrayer to frighten
s'élancer to rush forward
élever to erect; to bring up;
  s'élever to rise
emballer to wrap (up)
embrasser to kiss
emmener to take
empêcher (de) to prevent (from)
employer to use
emporter to take
emprunter qch à qn to borrow sth from sb
encourager qn à faire to encourage sb to do
s'endormir to fall asleep
enfermer to imprison
s'enfuir to flee
enlever to take away; to take off
s'ennuyer to be bored
enregistrer to record
entasser to stack
entendre to hear;
  qu'entendez-vous par...? what do you mean by ...?;
  entendre parler de to hear about;
  s'entendre to agree
entourer (de) to surround (with)
entrer (dans) to go *or* come in(to)
envahir to invade
envelopper to wrap (up)

envoyer to send
épeler to spell
éprouver to experience
espérer to hope
essayer (de faire qch) to try
  (to do sth)
essuyer to wipe
établir to establish, to set up
étaler to spread out
éteindre to put out; to switch off
s'étendre to stretch out
étonner to astonish;
  s'étonner to be astonished
étouffer to suffocate
être to be;
  être d'accord to agree;
  être assis(e) to be sitting;
  être obligé(e) de to be obliged to;
  être sur le point de to be just
  about to;
  être de retour to be back;
  être en train de faire qch to be
  doing sth
étudier to study
(s')éveiller to wake up
éviter (de faire) to avoid (doing)
exagérer to exaggerate
examiner to examine
s'excuser (de) to apologize (for)
exister to exist
expliquer to explain
exprimer to express
fabriquer to make
se fâcher to become angry
faillir: il a failli tomber
  he almost fell
faire to do; to make;

faire attention to be careful;
faire la bise à qn to kiss sb on the
cheek;
faire chaud/froid to be hot/cold;
faire la connaissance de to meet;
faire entrer quelqu'un to let
somebody in;
se faire couper les cheveux
to have one's hair cut;
faire halte to stop;
faire du mal (à) to harm;
faire partie de to belong to;
faire la queue to queue;
faire de son mieux (pour) to do
one's best (to);
faire une promenade to go for a
walk;
faire semblant de to pretend to;
faire signe to signal, to wave; **faire
un stage** to go on a training course
falloir to be necessary;
  il faut one must
féliciter to congratulate
fermer to close, to shut;
  fermer à clef to lock
se figurer to imagine
finir to finish
fixer to stare at; to fix
flâner to stroll
fonctionner to work;
  faire fonctionner to operate
former to form
fouiller to search
fournir to provide
frapper to hit, to knock
fréquenter to frequent; to see
gagner to win; to earn
garantir to guarantee

garder to keep

gâter to spoil;
  se gâter to go wrong

gémir to groan

gêner to bother

glisser to slip, to slide

gratter to scratch

grimper to climb

guetter to watch

habiter to live (in)

s'habituer à to get used to

hésiter to hesitate

heurter to bump into

ignorer not to know

imaginer to imagine

imprimer to print

indiquer qch à qn to inform sb
  of sth

s'inquiéter to worry

inscrire to note down;
  s'inscrire to register

installer to put in;
  s'installer to settle

s'instruire to educate oneself

insulter to insult

interdire to prohibit;
  "interdit de fumer"
  "no smoking"

intéresser to interest;
  s'intéresser à qch to be interested
  in sth

interroger to question

interrompre to interrupt

interviewer to interview

introduire to introduce

inventer to invent

inviter to invite

jeter to throw (away)

joindre to join

jurer to swear

laisser to leave; to let; to allow;
  laisser tomber to drop

lancer to throw

(se) laver to wash

lever to lift; to raise;
  se lever to get up; to stand up

lire to read

loger (chez) to live (with)

louer to hire, to rent

lutter to struggle

manœuvrer to operate

manquer to miss; to be lacking

marcher to walk; to work

se marier (avec qn) to marry (sb)

marquer to mark; to write down;
  to score

mêler to mix; **se mêler (à qch)**
  to get involved (in sth)

menacer to threaten

mener to lead

mentir to lie

mériter to deserve

mesurer to measure

mettre to put (on); to take;
  mettre qch au point to finalize
  sth; to perfect sth;
  mettre qn à la porte to throw
  sb out;
  se mettre à l'abri to take shelter;
  se mettre en colère to get angry;
  se mettre en route to set off

monter to come or go up;
  to get into

montrer to show

se moquer de to make fun of
mordre to bite
multiplier to multiply
noter to write down; to mark
nourrir to feed
obliger qn à faire to force sb to do
observer to observe; to keep
obtenir to obtain, to get
s'occuper de to attend to
offrir to give
s'opposer à to be opposed to
ordonner to order
organiser to organize
orner (de) to decorate (with)
oser (faire qch) to dare (to do sth)
oublier to forget
ouvrir to open
paraître to appear
parier (sur) to bet (on)
parler to speak, to talk
partager to share
participer (à) to take part (in)
partir to leave, to go away
passer to pass; to spend (*time*);
  passer un examen to sit an exam;
  se passer to happen
passionner to fascinate
payer to pay
peindre to paint
pénétrer (dans) to enter
penser (à) to think (about)
perdre to lose;
  perdre qn de vue to lose sight
  of sb
permettre (à qn de faire)
  to allow (sb to do)
persuader to persuade

peser to weigh
photographier to photograph
placer to place, to put
se plaindre (de) to complain (about)
plaire (à) to please;
  cela me plaît I like that
plaisanter to joke
pleurer to cry
plier to fold
porter to carry; to wear; to take
poser to put (down);
  poser des questions to ask
  questions
posséder to own
poursuivre to pursue
pousser to push; to grow
pouvoir to be able to
pratiquer to play; to practise
précipiter to hurl;
  se précipiter dans to rush into
prédire to predict
préférer to prefer
prendre to take;
  prendre qch à qn to take sth
  from sb;
  prendre part à to take part in;
  prendre soin (de) to take care (to)
préparer to prepare
présenter to present; to introduce;
  se présenter to appear;
  to introduce oneself
prêter qch à qn to lend sb sth
prévoir to foresee
prier to request;
  je vous en prie please, don't
  mention it
priver qn de qch to deprive sb of sth

produire to produce;
  se produire to happen
profiter (de) to take advantage (of)
se promener to go for a walk
promettre (à qn de faire qch)
  to promise (sb to do sth)
prononcer to pronounce
proposer (de faire) to suggest
  (doing)
protéger to protect
protester to protest
prouver to prove
provoquer to cause
se quereller to quarrel
quitter to leave
raccommoder to mend
raconter to tell
ralentir to slow down
ramasser to pick up
ramener to bring or take back
ranger to tidy
se rappeler to remember
rapporter to report; to bring back
rassurer to reassure
rater to miss; to fail
rattraper qn to catch up with sb
recevoir to receive
réchauffer to warm (up)
recommander to recommend;
  to register
recommencer to begin again
reconnaître to recognize
recouvrir (de) to cover (with)
reculer to move back; to reverse
redescendre to come or go down
  again
refaire to do again

refermer to close again
réfléchir to think
refuser (de) to refuse (to)
regagner to go back to
regarder to look (at)
régler to adjust; to settle
regretter (que) to be sorry (that)
rejoindre to join; to catch up
se relever to get up again
relier to connect
relire to read again
remarquer to notice
rembourser to refund
remercier (de) to thank (for)
remettre to put back; to postpone
remplacer to replace
remplir (de) to fill (with)
remuer to stir
rencontrer to meet;
  se rencontrer to meet
rendre to give back;
  rendre visite à to visit;
  se rendre to give oneself up;
  se rendre à to visit;
  se rendre compte to realize
renseigner to inform;
  se renseigner (sur) to inquire
  (about)
rentrer to go back (in)
renverser to run over;
  to spill; to knock over
renvoyer to expel, to dismiss;
  to send back
réparer to repair
repasser to iron
répéter to repeat
répondre to answer

se reposer to rest
reprendre to resume
représenter to represent
réserver to book
résoudre to solve
respecter to respect
ressembler à to look like
rester to stay
retenir to book
retourner to return;
  se retourner to turn round
retrouver to meet; to find (again)
se réunir to meet
réussir (à faire) to succeed
  (in doing)
réveiller to wake up;
  se réveiller to wake up
révéler to reveal
revenir to come back
rêver to dream
revoir to see again;
  au revoir goodbye
rire to laugh
risquer (de) to risk
rougir to blush
rouler to drive (along)
saisir to grasp
salir to dirty
saluer to greet
sauter to jump
sauver to save;
  se sauver to run off
savoir to know
sécher to dry
secouer to shake
sélectionner to select
sembler to seem

sentir to smell; to feel;
  se sentir (mal) to feel (ill)
séparer to separate
serrer to tighten;
  se serrer la main to shake hands
se servir to help oneself;
  se servir de qch to use sth
siffler to whistle
signaler to point out
signer to sign
soigner to look after
sonner to ring
sortir to go or come out;
  to take out
se soucier de to worry about
souffrir to suffer
souhaiter to wish
soulager to relieve
soulever to lift
soupçonner to suspect
soupirer to sigh
sourire to smile
se souvenir de qch to remember sth
sucer to suck
suffire to be sufficient
suggérer to suggest
suivre to follow
supposer to suppose
surprendre to surprise
sursauter to jump
se taire to be quiet;
  taisez-vous! be quiet!
téléphoner (à) to phone
tendre to hold out
tenir to hold
tenter de to attempt to
(se) terminer to finish

tirer to pull; to shoot
tomber to fall;
 laisser tomber to drop;
 tomber en panne to break down
toucher to touch
tourner to turn; to shoot;
 se tourner vers to turn towards
traduire to translate
trahir to betray
traîner to drag
travailler to work
traverser to cross; to go through;
 to go over
trembler to shake
tricher to cheat
tromper to deceive;
 se tromper to be mistaken
troubler to worry
trouver to find;
 se trouver to be situated

tuer to kill
unir to unite
utiliser to use
vaincre to conquer
valoir to be worth
vendre to sell
venir to come;
 venir de faire qch to have just
 done sth
vérifier to check
verser to pour
visiter to visit
vivre to live
voir to see
voler to steal; to fly
vouloir to want;
 vouloir bien faire to be happy
 to do;
 vouloir dire to mean
voyager to travel

ENGLISH
INDEX

The words on the following pages cover all of the ESSENTIAL
and IMPORTANT NOUNS in the book.

Printed in the USA
CPSIA information can be obtained
at www.ICGtesting.com
LVHW032150191223
766958LV00049B/1492